# Hospital Tramways and Railways

by David Voice

SECOND EDITION

Published by Adam Gordon

**ALSO BY DAVID VOICE**
How to Go Tram and Tramway Modelling
London's Tramways and How to Model Them
What Colour was that Tram?
Tramway Modelling in 'OO' Gauge
More Tramway Modelling in 'OO' Gauge
The Illustrated History of Kidderminster and Stourport Electric Tramway Company
(with Melvyn Thompson)
How to Go Tram and Tramway Modelling, 2nd edition
The Millennium Guide to Trams in the British Isles
The Definitive Guide to Trams in the British Isles, 2nd edition
The Definitive Guide to Trams in the British Isles, 3rd edition
Toy and Model Trams of the World, Volume 1: Toys, Die-casts and Souvenirs (with Gottfried Kuře)
Toy and Model Trams of the World, Volume 2: Plastic, White Metal and Brass (with Gottfried Kuře)
Next Stop Seaton! (with David Jay)
How to Go Tram and Tramway Modelling, 3rd edition
Hospital Tramways and Railways 1st edition

2nd enlarged Edition
© David Voice 2006
All rights reserved. No part of this publication may be reproduced, stored in a retrieval system or transmitted in any form or by any means electronic, mechanical, photocopying, recording or otherwise, without prior permission in writing from the author David Voice.
British Library Cataloguing in Publication Data
Voice, David
Hospital Tramways and Railways

ISBN 1-874422-63-X (978-1-874422-63-1)
Publication no. 67
Published in 2005 by Adam Gordon, Kintradwell Farm, Brora, Sutherland KW9 6LU
Tel: 01408 622660
E-mail: adam@adamgordon.freewire.co.uk
First printing limited to 300 copies
First printing of second edition limited to 300 copies

Printed by: 4edge Ltd., 7a Eldon Way, Eldon Way Industrial Estate, Hockley, Essex SS5 4AD
Production by: Trevor Preece, 2 Sella Bank, The Banks, Seascale, Cumbria CA20 1QU
E-mail: trevor@epic.gb.com

# CONTENTS

**BACKGROUND** ..........................................................................................................................................................4

**INTRODUCTION** .......................................................................................................................................................5

## ENGLISH HOSPITAL TRAMWAYS AND RAILWAYS

Addenbrookes Hospital ..................................................................................................................................................7
Calderstones Hospital ....................................................................................................................................................7
Christ's Hospital ............................................................................................................................................................8
Cumberland and Westmorland Convalescent Institution ..............................................................................................8
Epsom Hospitals Complex ..........................................................................................................................................11
Haslar Royal Naval Hospital .......................................................................................................................................13
Hellingly Hospital .......................................................................................................................................................14
High Royds Hospital ...................................................................................................................................................16
Hollymoor Hospital .....................................................................................................................................................17
Joyce Green Hospital ..................................................................................................................................................19
Knowle Hospital ..........................................................................................................................................................20
Lord Mayor Treloars Hospital.....................................................................................................................................22
Netley Military Hospital .............................................................................................................................................24
Park Prewett Hospital..................................................................................................................................................26
Queen Mary's Hospital for Children...........................................................................................................................28
Royal Lancaster Infirmary ..........................................................................................................................................29
St Edward's Hospital...................................................................................................................................................30
Scalebor Park Hospital ................................................................................................................................................32
Three Counties Hospital..............................................................................................................................................33
Whittingham Hospital .................................................................................................................................................36

## WAR-TIME TEMPORARY MILITARY HOSPITALS IN ENGLAND

Introduction ................................................................................................................................................................39

Bewdley USA Military Hospital.................................................................................................................................41
Bulford Camp Military Hospital .................................................................................................................................43
Codford Camp Military Hospital ................................................................................................................................47
Fargo Military Hospital...............................................................................................................................................47
Fovant Camp Military Hospital...................................................................................................................................50
Ingress Abbey Hospital ...............................................................................................................................................51
Morley US Military Hospital ......................................................................................................................................53
Sutton Veny Camp Military Hospital..........................................................................................................................54
Tidworth Camp Military Hospital...............................................................................................................................56

## SCOTTISH HOSPITAL TRAMWAYS AND RAILWAYS

Introduction ................................................................................................................................................................60

Bangour Hospital.........................................................................................................................................................60
Dykebar Hospital.........................................................................................................................................................63
Glasgow Royal Infirmary ............................................................................................................................................64
Hartwood Hospital ......................................................................................................................................................65
Ladysbridge Hospital ..................................................................................................................................................67
Lennox Castle Hospital ...............................................................................................................................................67
Murthly Hospital .........................................................................................................................................................69
Rosslynlee Hospital.....................................................................................................................................................70
Royal Scottish National Hospital ................................................................................................................................71

## WELSH HOSPITAL RAILWAY

Prince of Wales Hospital, Rhydlafar ...........................................................................................................................73

**ACKNOWLEDGEMENTS AND SOURCES**..........................................................................................................74

# BACKGROUND

## HEALTHCARE

The National Health Service is close to the hearts of the British people. Most people in the country have been in a hospital at one time or other. Newspapers are full of health stories, many of which are about hospitals. Indeed we are so used to our hospitals that it comes as a shock to realise that in terms of human development hospitals are a very recent innovation.

The idea of having special places for those that are ill or injured has a long history. The Romans built special temples devoted to the treatment of people who were ill. Of course this only applied to the wealthy. The general population and particularly slaves had to rely on themselves or their families for help. Indeed one lesser known Roman fact is that ill or handicapped babies would be 'exposed', that is left out, usually on the town rubbish tip, to die.

After the Roman Empire collapsed, hospitals disappeared. Communities would have someone who knew about the healing properties of herbs and other remedies and these individuals would provide a form of healthcare. The hospital concept was used again by monasteries, a tradition that was well developed by the Middle Ages. They would treat the ill or injured, and some monks became very proficient in the growing and gathering of medicinal herbs and plants. In those days illness was associated with faith, with the theory that a healthy soul was necessary for a healthy body.

Gradually there was a shift from monks to doctors for the treatment of the sick. Mixed in with this is the role of barbers. It was believed that illness could be cured by blood letting and barbers, with their sharp razors, were well placed to provide the service. They expanded their role to encompass minor operations and this became the beginnings of surgery. This is why there is a tradition where a doctor is called 'Doctor', but if they further qualify as a surgeon they revert back to being called 'Mr'.

In the Georgian age more hospitals opened, under the management of doctors. The Government started to become involved and in 1808 the Lunacy Act empowered counties to build asylums using money raised through the rates. Previously all hospitals were built with either private money or by raising public donations for the hospital. From the Victorian age to the first half of the 20th century hospitals fell into two categories, 'Private' and 'Public'. Actually neither was free, but the 'Public' hospitals were generally less expensive than the 'Private'.

In 1948 the Government created the National Health Service and took over the management and control of most hospitals. The reason for the State controlling and funding health care was the recognition that many people were unable to gain access to health care. Generally the working man was covered by his employer's insurance schemes. But wives at home (when women married they were bound by community expectation and their employers to leave any job they had in order to look after their husbands and raise a family) did not have such cover. Many suffered from debilitating illnesses with no hope of health care as their family could not afford the medical expenses. The 1947 NHS Act was passed to meet this need.

In 1948 it was expected that there would be a surge of patients taking advantage of free health care and then the demand would slacken to pre NHS levels, or lower, as people became more fit from their health care. Indeed there was an initial surge and the demand then fell back a little, but nowhere back to the previous levels. What happened was that health expectations started to rise. Medical developments and their publicity in the media (particularly recently television) have fed this expectation. So today we demand an instant cure or relieving operation for most illnesses or injuries we suffer. It has been recognised that no matter how well the NHS performs, the expectations of the public will always outpace the ability to meet the demands.

## HOSPITAL TRAMWAYS AND RAILWAYS

Only a few hospitals had their own tramway or railway. So why should this small number get such a transport link? It really comes down to a number of factors needing to be present. The hospital had to be built in the latter half of the 19th century or the first half of the 20th century. It needed to be large. The hospital would need to be located in a very rural area with limited road access and it would need to be reasonably close to an existing railway line. Such hospitals were complete towns in their own right, with their own farms. Produce cultivated on the farms was used not only for feeding the patients and staff, but also for selling on the open market (the income provided by the farm was a major contribution to reducing the costs of the hospitals on the rate payers). The hospitals had their own bakery, brewery, laundry, tailors, kitchens and hairdressers. They produced their own gas, heating and electricity. They undertook most of the repairs and maintenance of the building and equipment. There were also all kinds of recreational facilities. Usually there were cricket football and hockey teams. There would be a theatre offering productions to patients, staff and visitors. Dances were a regular feature for the staff.

The hospitals most likely to have their own tramway or railway were the large mental health units that were built outside the town or city boundaries. Often the line came about when the hospital was built. The building contractor would lay a railway line to connect the site with the railway network. Then the tons of building materials needed would be delivered by rail. For example when St Edwards Hospital was built there were 500 workers on site; the buildings used 18 million bricks; a complete sewage disposal system had to be built; four massive Lancashire boilers (each 30ft by 7ft 6in) were installed in the boiler house; a 100ft deep well was dug; and a 36,000 gallon water tank mounted at the top of a 135ft tower.

When such a hospital was completed the contractor's railway was often converted to the hospital tramway or railway. The main purpose of the line would be the delivery of coal to the boiler house. It was not unusual for such a hospital to use 200 tons of coal a month. The line would also bring produce for the kitchens and often a passenger service of sorts was established for staff and visitors. Strangely there are some hospitals where a contractor's railway was built but was removed on completion of the hospital and the hospital ran without the advantage of a rail link.

Two Acts of Parliament led to a number of large mental health hospitals being built in the latter half of the 19th Century. In 1845 the Act for the Regulation, Care and Treatment of Lunatics required each county to provide an asylum for the care of its pauper lunatics. Then in 1853 an Act prohibited the use of any form of restraining device on lunatics in Workhouses. So there was pressure for all the poor mentally ill to be cared for in hospitals run by the counties funded by the rates. These hospitals were built in the countryside. This was not, as many believe, to remove the mentally ill from the community. There were several reasons for locating the hospitals outside urban areas. Part of the treatment programme included encouraging the patients to participate in running a farm. This was partly as

# INTRODUCTION

therapy, particularly in the fresh air, and partly to provide fresh fruit and vegetables for the hospital and an income stream from produce being sold. The second reason was that land was less expensive, a key point when the size of the hospital and its farm was taken into account. Finally doctors were of the opinion that the fresh air of the countryside was a key factor in the treatment of the ill.

Hospital railways and tramways provided a valuable service for many years. However, the end of hospital tramways and railways came in the 1950s and 1960s. The then Government had a new policy of converting hospital boilers to oil firing rather than coal. This was an enormous task and took over a decade to complete. Once the hospitals had their boiler houses converted the need for vast amounts of coal disappeared. Instead a road oil tanker would deliver the fuel. Thus the reign of the hospital tramway and railway came to an end. This was around the very beginnings of the transport preservation movement, so enthusiasts would often arrange a visit to ride on the railway a few months before it closed. But there was no concerted effort to preserve the lines or any of the equipment. So they disappeared with little or no trace.

In more recent times the attitude to the care of the ill, particularly the mentally ill, has changed considerably. The Government initiative "Care in the Community" encouraged the assimilation of those with psychiatric disorders into the general community. The day of the large institution caring for thousands of patients was gone. Over a surprisingly short period patients were moved out of the hospitals into community care. This left large buildings and tracts of land surplus to NHS requirements. By this time most of the hospitals were no longer in rural environments. The towns or cities had grown to surround them. So the land and buildings were sold for housing, retail or industrial use.

I have been interested in tramways and railways ever since I can remember. I grew up in South London and I can just remember the trams. Routes 8, 10, 20, 22 and 24 ran along the street at the bottom of my road. Later I used the green Southern Electric Trains when I commuted to and from the centre of London. Throughout this time I also had a deep interest in railway and later tramway modelling.

My career took me from London into the Health Service via a spell in engineering. For many years my work and hobby were quite separate. But I discovered that a few hospitals used to have their own tramway or railway. This fascinated me and I started to acquire information on these unusual lines.

Recently I have had time to undertake a more detailed look into the subject. This has led me into a vastly larger arena than I had ever expected. Indeed at one stage I wondered if I would ever reach an end to the number of hospitals that were closely associated with tramways and railways. In particular I discovered a whole new area where there were links between railway lines and wartime temporary Military Hospitals.

I felt that it would help you when reading the book to group the hospitals geographically, except for the temporary Military Hospitals, which have a chapter to themselves. I have not found any links between hospitals and tramways or railways in Ireland.

## NOTE

In earlier days the names of the hospitals and stations often used words that are no longer felt to be acceptable. For historical record I have kept to the original names in use at the time being described.

## INTRODUCTION TO SECOND EDITION

When the first edition of the book was published the numbers sold surprised both the publisher and me. I had never expected that there were so many people who were also interested in this small branch of tramway and railway history. There was also considerable correspondence from readers offering additional information and detail about the lines. There were some hospitals with rail connections that had been missed from the first edition. This new edition now incorporates the additional information and details on those hospitals not included in the previous book.

*David Voice*
*March 2006*

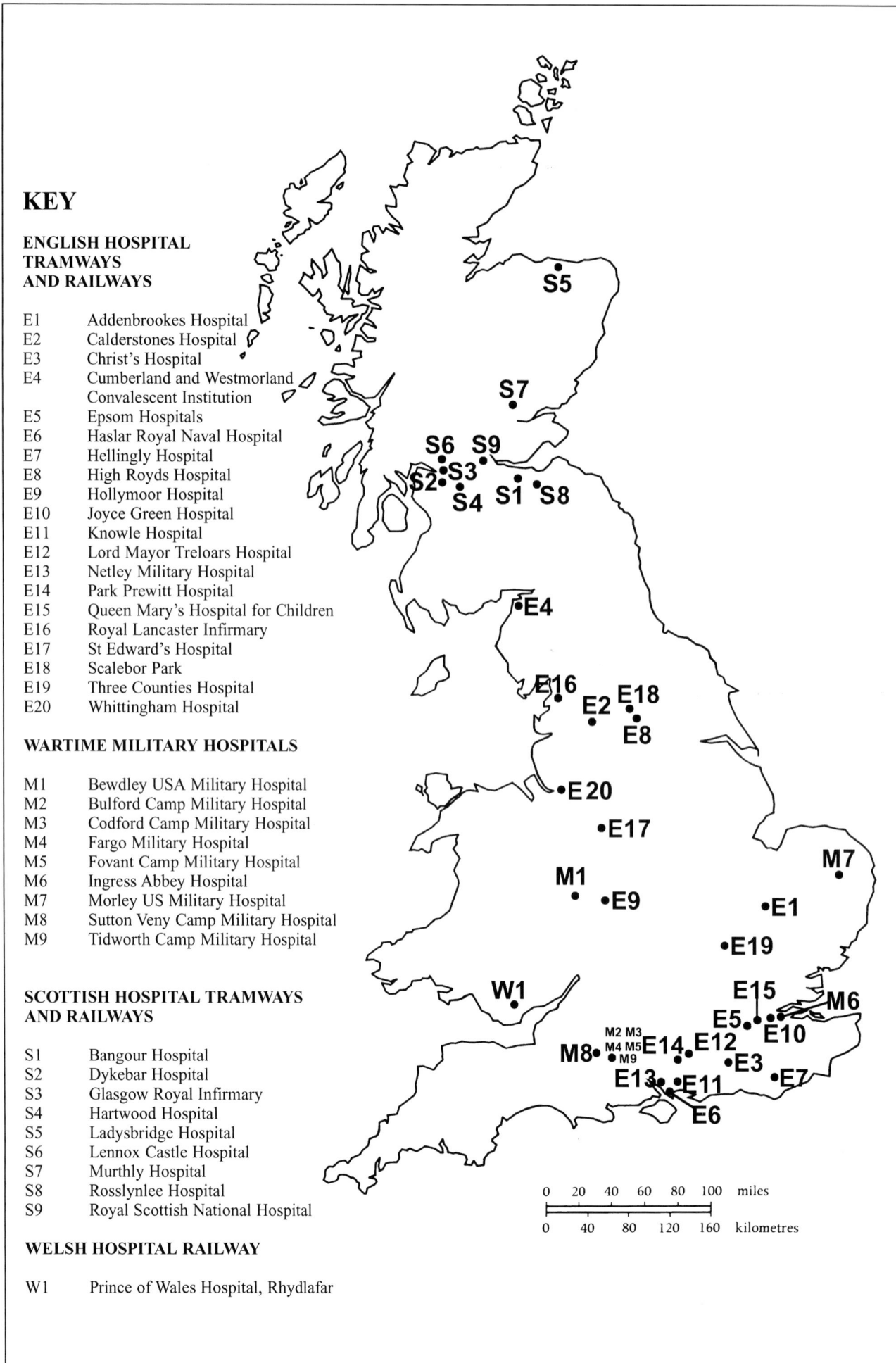

# ENGLISH HOSPITAL TRAMWAYS AND RAILWAYS

## ADDENBROOKES HOSPITAL

The famous Addenbrookes Hospital in Cambridge is justly known for its specialist health care. Located in the southern part of the city, close to the main railway line, the hospital has only road transport links. Public transport and parking for staff and visitors is always a problem. In the 1990s the local authority examined proposals for building a station near Addenbrookes Hospital to serve the hospital and the southern part of Cambridge. In 2002, following settlement development north of Cambridge at Waterbeach, the developers and the local railway operator proposed a rail expansion, doubling the track between Waterbeach and Addenbrookes Hospital, building three new stations at Waterbeach, Chesterton and Addenbrookes Hospital. The line would include the existing stations at Waterbeach and Cambridge. A rail shuttle would be provided between the furthest stations. However, in 2004 the Local Authority dropped the idea of developing the railway and instead built a new bus station near the hospital. However, the idea may, one day, be resurrected.

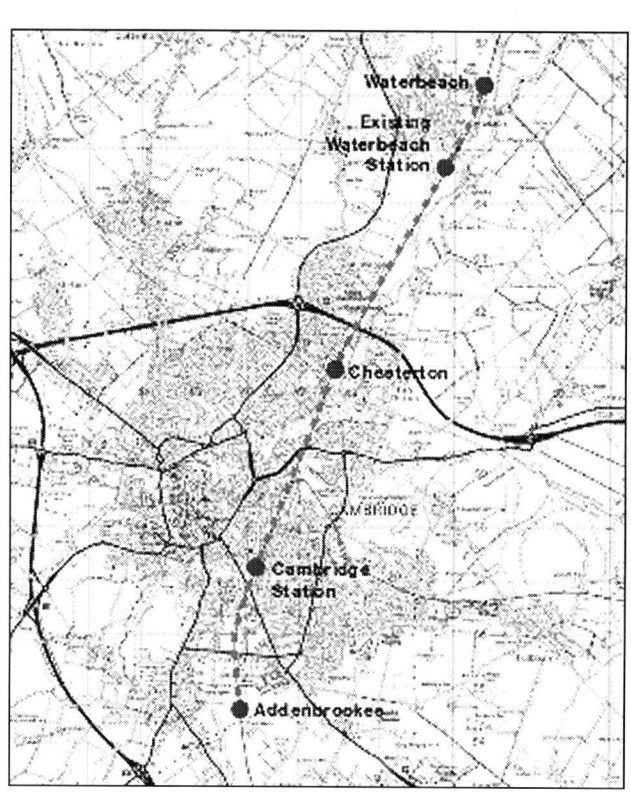

The proposal for an improved commuter rail service for Cambridge and a new station at Addenbrookes Hospital.

## CALDERSTONES HOSPITAL

*Also known as:*
**Queen Mary's Military Hospital.**
**Calderstone's Certified Institution for Mental Defectives.**
**Whalley Asylum**

In 1901 the Lancashire Asylums Board agreed to build a second mental health hospital for the county, the first being Brockhall Hospital, just two miles from the Calderstones site. The process was somewhat prolonged and it was not until 1906 that land was acquired near Whalley, between Blackburn and Clitheroe. Work on the site started in 1907 with R. Neill & Sons as the contractor at a cost of £355,848. However, it seems that opportunity was taken while the site was being landscaped to use the clay to make bricks. The Ordnance Survey maps for 1912 shows a brickworks on the site with a half mile long private siding connected to the Lancashire and

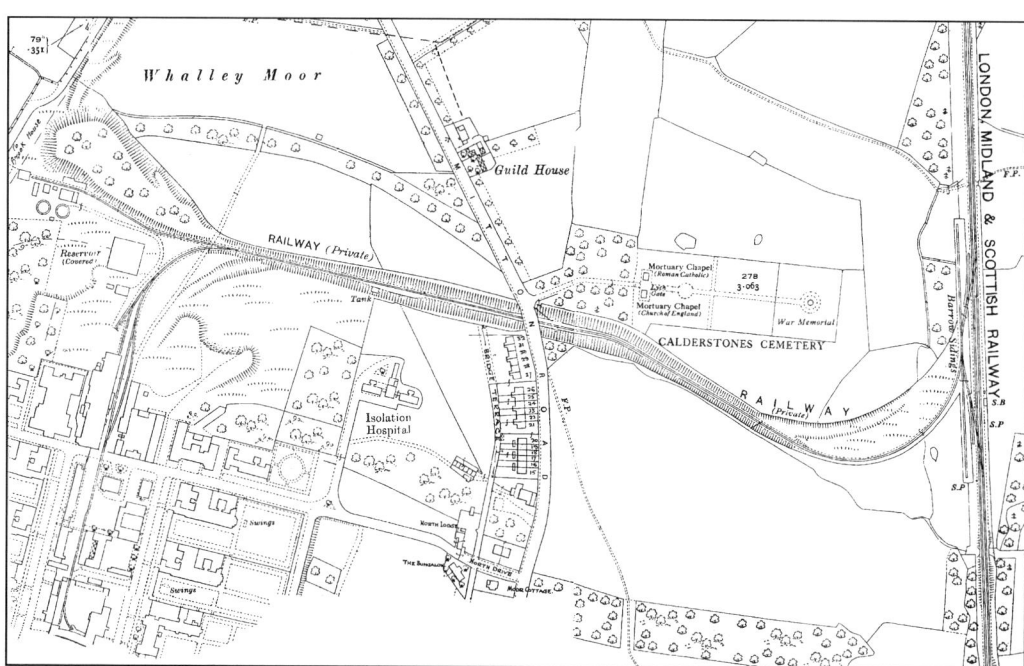

Calderstones Hospital railway. Ordnance Survey map 1932.

7

Calderstones Hospital platforms in the grounds. The double platform allowed patients to be moved to the wards as quickly as possible.

Yorkshire Railway (later London Midland and Scottish) Bolton, Blackburn and Hellifield line just south of Whalley station. There were transfer sidings alongside the main line and then a single track led across open country along the north boundary of the hospital site. There was also a two-foot gauge system used on the site, using an 0-4-2 saddle tank locomotive called "Claretoi". The railway was probably aligned according to the needs of each stage of building. Unfortunately R. Neill & Sons was liquidated in 1911 and the contract was taken over by Parkinson & Sons of Blackpool. The fabric of the hospital was completed towards the end of 1914. By this time the country had entered the First World War and the building was offered on loan to the War Office as a military hospital. The hospital was formally opened in April 1915 and was named Queen Mary's Military Hospital with a capacity of 2,110 beds. The private railway link was extended south to reach the power house so that coal could be delivered directly to the boilers. Advantage was taken of the railway link and a station was built close to the wards to enable the transfer of wounded troops with the minimum inconvenience to them. The station had wooden platforms either side of a single track. Long gentle ramps were provided at the ends. At the same time the sharp curve leading from the main line had to be realigned to allow the coaches of the hospital trains to negotiate the curve. The original embankment can be seen on the map. The first wounded arrived at the hospital in May 1915. Calderstones Cemetery was built on land north of the private railway to take soldiers who did not recover in the hospital. Later a war memorial was erected at one end of the cemetery.

Although hostilities ceased in 1918 the hospital remained under military control until 1921 when it was returned to the Lancashire Asylums Board and renamed The Calderstones Certified Institution for Mental Defectives. Later it was called Whalley Asylum. By this time the hospital could accommodate around 3,000 patients and employed some 1,000 staff.

The private railway continued in use for goods traffic, mainly coal for the boilers. There is no record of the line being used by passengers, patients or staff. With the collapse of R. Neill & Sons the County Council took over the two standard gauge locomotives, a 1911 0-4-0 saddle tank named "Walley" and an 1890 0-6-0 saddle tank called "Thornhill". They were both sold to Parkinson & Sons for use during the completion of the hospital. It is likely that "Walley" was kept by the hospital for internal shunting. It was replaced in 1925 by a new 0-4-0 locomotive

"Farnham Slade". This was renamed "Calderstones", probably around 1929 when the name Calderstones Hospital came in use.

In the 1990s, following the changes in approach to mental care, the hospital became surplus to needs. After a few years of planned reduction, the hospital had virtually closed by 1993. Just a 211-bedded regional medium secure unit was retained. The rest of the site was demolished and a housing development called "Calderstones Park" was built on the site.

Its final claim to fame is that Calderstones Hospital has been recognised as being the very centre of mainland Britain.

# CHRIST'S HOSPITAL

There is a railway station in West Sussex, near Arundel, called Christ's Hospital. However, that name refers to a school and not a hospital. So no further details are given.

# CUMBERLAND AND WESTMORLAND CONVALESCENT INSTITUTION

*Also known as:*
**Silloth Nursing and Residential Care Home**

Silloth is a coastal resort in the North West with the Solway Firth on one side and the Lake District on the other. The name is believed to derive from Sea Lathes (barns for grain storage that are beside the sea). It is some eighteen miles east of Carlisle. Now a popular seaside resort it has a population of almost 3,000, originally a small settlement promoted by the monks of Holme Cultram Abbey, who encouraged local folk to farm the land and to help with the monks' salt industry.

In the early 1800s a move was made by Carlisle businessmen to find a less expensive means of importing their raw materials, mainly cotton, and shipping out the finished goods. The goods

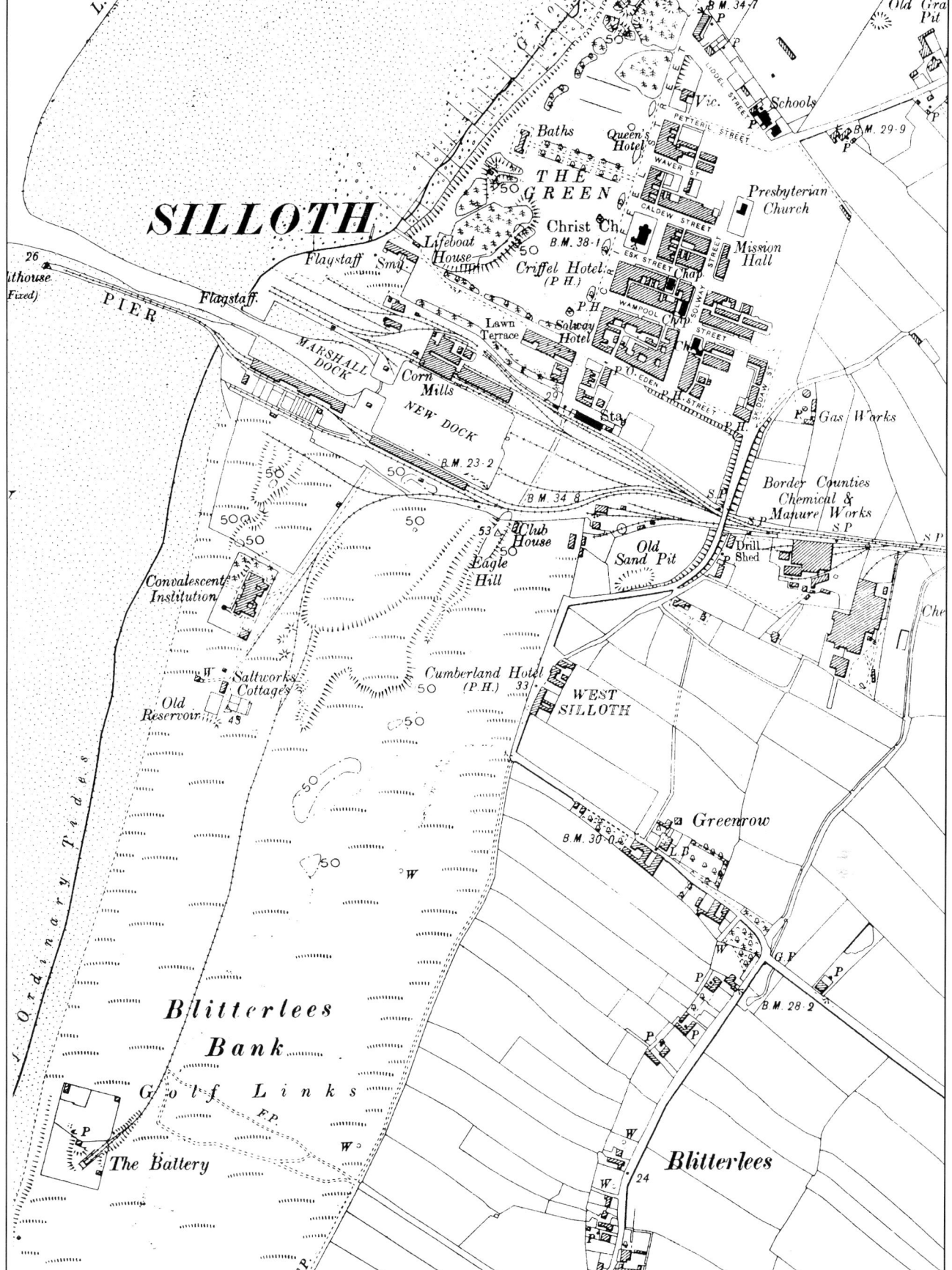

The siding to the Convalescent Institute branches off the longer line to the gun battery. Ordnance Survey map 1901.

were all passing through Liverpool docks with a costly land journey to Carlisle. In 1819 work began on building a canal between Carlisle and Port Carlisle about eleven miles from the city. It opened in 1823. However, the coming of the railways soon saw the demise of the canal. The canal route was converted into the Carlisle and Port Carlisle Railway (C&PCR) in 1854. However, it was only a partial answer to the businessmen's problems. This was because the sea access to Port Carlisle was restricted to a couple of hours on each tide and there were major problems with silting of the channel. Ships unable to dock would

The only photograph I have found of the Convalescent Institute and the railway. Taken about 1904 the view shows the platform and North British Railway coaches.

wait in Silloth Bay, where there was shelter from adverse weather.

It was realised that if a dock was built at Silloth it would be accessible at all times and give safe anchorage for ships. The businessmen raised the necessary capital for building the docks, a one thousand foot long pier and a railway, the Carlisle and Silloth Bay Railway (C&SBR) linking with the C&PCR. The line opened in 1856. A new hotel and other buildings had been constructed to serve the expected traffic. However, the dock was not opened until 1859, so the backers of the line encouraged use of the railway during these three years, promoting the hamlet as a holiday resort. Once the dock had opened they found that the expected volume of goods traffic did not materialise. The North Eastern Railway Company (NER) had diverted traffic from North East England away from Carlisle, taking a route to Liverpool via York and Bolton. This had a very serious financial effect on the C&SBR, with takings well below forecasts and the company was effectively insolvent in 1861.

The immense investment in the railway and docks seemed a lost cause. However, the North British Railway Company (NBR) leased the C&PCR and the C&SBR for 999 years in 1862. This was the only example of a Scottish railway company running a line entirely in England. The NBR had the power to divert Scottish traffic onto the Silloth line and to the new port for shipping to Liverpool. Indeed the increase was such they also formed their own Steam Packet Company to sail out of Silloth.

At Silloth Station the line split with one branch going south of the dock to sidings and the pier while the other went to the north and the station itself. Soon after the railway opened a line was laid from the southern sidings to Leesworth Salt Works.

At the same time in 1862, as the railway was taken over by the North British Railway, the Cumberland and Westmorland Convalescence Institution was opened, located south of the station. The aim was to provide an opportunity for those poor with a fever to recuperate in the pure Silloth air. An eminent physician declared "the air of Silloth to be cleaner and more health giving than anywhere else". The convalescent home was built alongside the sidings leading to the Salt Works. A wooden platform was built to allow coaches to be shunted down the siding to the home. This was particularly helpful for the invalids going to the Home. As a gesture of goodwill the NBR gave the Home 60 free passes for return trips from Carlisle to Silloth. The trip along the siding to the Home must have been memorable. The line was unfenced and so a man with a red flag would have to walk in front of the train, ensuring that the line was clear for the train.

The home was extended in 1882 when a children's ward was built. In 1886 a gunnery battery was opened south of the convalescence home. A branch siding was added, starting from just before the convalescent home, going south to the battery. The battery was built by Armstrong Whitworth to test guns with ranges of up to four miles. Various dignitaries would be taken out to the battery to see guns being tested.

The Salt Works closed in 1890, having been purchased by the NBR. They announced that they would close the siding to the Salt Works and the Convalescent Home. However the Board of Governors of the Home persuaded the NBR to leave enough of the siding to continue to allow access to the Home.

The gunnery battery was in use until 1928, when a new range was opened in Eskmeals, nearer to the Vickers works at Barrow. The Silloth battery then closed. It is likely that traffic on the sidings ceased from this time.

Silloth Station. The branch to the Convalescent Institution and the gun battery is the line on the furthest left of the photograph.

23 October 1950 saw a major accident on the line. The 1.15pm train from Carlisle to Silloth derailed between Drumburgh Junction and Kirkbride. The locomotive and tender parted from the carriages and plunged into the peat field alongside the track. It overturned with fatal consequences for the driver and fireman. Of the 24 passengers in the coaches just three were slightly hurt. The Board of Trade carried out an investigation and blamed the poor condition of the track for the accident. This led to British Railways re-laying the track with heavier rail and concrete sleepers.

The Silloth branch was listed for closure by Dr Beeching in 1963. It had been declining in business and the cost of maintenance and repairs was far in excess of the passenger traffic. Whilst holiday makers did fill the trains during summer weekends, the line was underused the rest of the time. Despite a vigorous campaign to keep the line open the last train ran in 1964.

It is not clear when the line to the convalescent home was closed. Whether it ceased when the battery moved in 1928, or whether it carried on carrying patients for longer is not known. The home itself still exists. It was registered as a charity in 1963 and is now called Silloth Nursing and Residential Care Home providing care and counselling to the elderly.

# EPSOM HOSPITALS COMPLEX

*Incorporating:*
**Epsom's Hospitals Railway**
**Ewell Epileptic Colony**
**Ewell Mental Hospital**
**Horton Light Railway**
**Horton Lunatic Asylum**
**Horton Hospital**
**Horton Manor Asylum**
**Long Grove Hospital**
**Long Grove Asylum**
**Long Grove Light Railway**
**Manor Hospital**
**St Ebba's Asylum for the Epileptic Insane**
**St Ebba's Hospital**
**West Park Hospital**

In 1890 the London County Council bought the Manor of Horton, with the intention to build a number of hospitals on the site to take mentally ill patients from London. The first, Horton Manor Asylum, was built in 1899. This was followed in 1901 by Horton Lunatic Asylum and in 1902 by St Ebba's Colony for the Epileptic Insane (at this time epilepsy was considered to be a form of insanity). While these were each large hospitals in their own right, the London County Council had plans for an even larger hospital. This was Long Grove Asylum and construction started in 1904. Vast quantities of building materials were carried to Epsom station and transported the last few miles by road. However, the rural nature of the hospital site meant that the roads were no more than country lanes. The building traffic caused an enormous nuisance and Epsom Council passed a byelaw restricting the use of locomotives on the highway to between the hours of 8.00pm and 6.00am. This was too much for the contractor and application was immediately made for permission to build a standard gauge light railway from Ewell Station (now known as Ewell West) and the Long Grove site, some one mile three furlongs long. It opened in 1905. The contractor had its own locomotive, an 0-6-0 saddle tank engine named "Hollymoor" that took goods wagons left at Ewell Station to the building site. Later a second engine "Crossness" was added. The building of the hospital was completed in 1907 and in normal circumstances the contractor's railway would have been removed. But the London County Council decided to purchase the line and the locomotive "Crossness", though it was clear at the time that the route would need to be realigned.

Part of the development of Long Grove Asylum included the building of a Central Pumping and Electric Light Plant. This was situated at an approximately equal distance from all the hospitals and was in addition to the boiler houses for heating at Long Grove and West Park Hospitals. The LCC decided that the new railway should serve Long Grove, the Central Pumping and Electric Light Works and the future West Park Hospital. Authority to build the

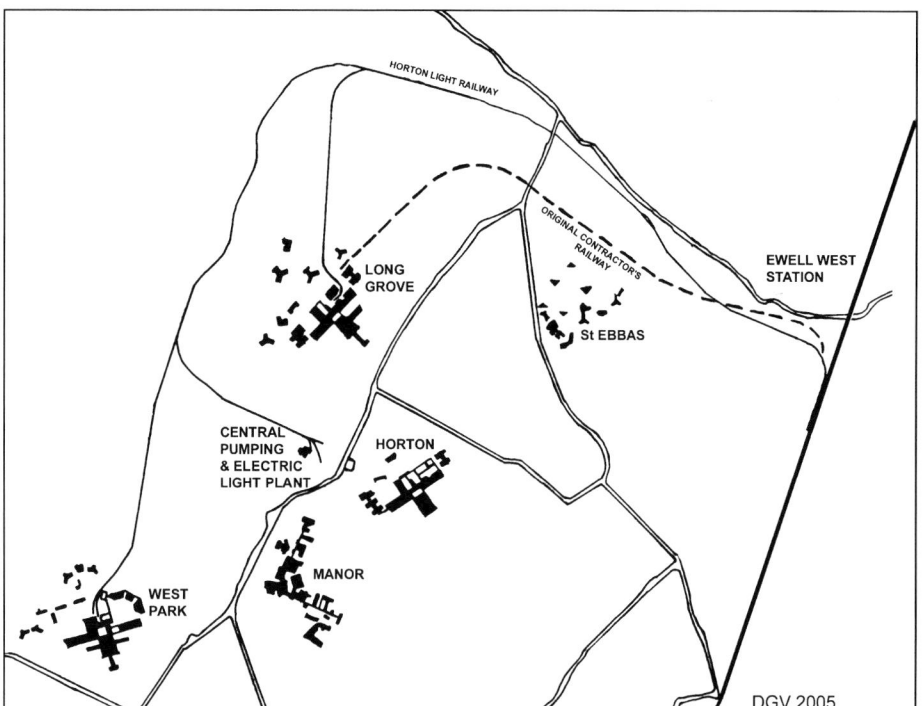

**The Epsom Hospitals complex with the original contractor's railway and the later Horton Light Railway. Based on a map by R.I. Essen.**

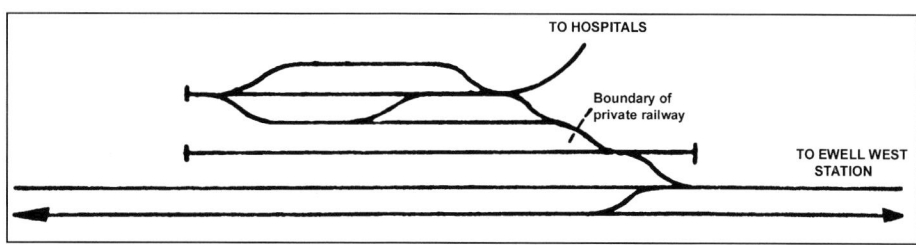

**The exchange sidings between the hospitals and the Southern Railway between Epsom and Ewell West stations.**

11

"Hendon" hauls a typical train of coal wagons over the Horton Light Railway.

three mile two furlongs line was applied for in 1908 and construction started a couple of years later. The new line started as before from Ewell Station but then followed a different route through the hospital grounds. An engine shed was built by the boiler house. By the time the new railway, now called the Horton Light Railway, opened the First World War had started.

Patients were moved from Horton Hospital and it was used to treat wounded soldiers from the Commonwealth. With the railway in place it was planned that ambulance trains would take the wounded directly from the South Coast ports to the hospital.

Looking across the main line railway to the Hospital exchange sidings near Ewell West Station.

However, when tests were done it was found that the tight curves and limited clearances meant that normal trains could not run along the line. Ambulance trains had to go to Epsom Station and patients would transfer to the hospital by road. The hospital railway continued to be used to carry coal to the boiler houses on the site. In 1916 King George V and Queen Mary visited the 2,000 military patients in the hospital.

After the War the railway was used to transport building materials for the new West Park Hospital that opened in 1921. By now the complex needed over 7,000 workers, which represented 20% of the population of Epsom. But for the railway the main business was with coal wagons. The trucks would be pushed from the rear and dropped off at Long Grove first, then West Park then going back to the Central Pumping House. The size of the complex is reflected in the amount of coal used. Around 15,000 tons of coal were burnt each year. Although the original contractor's railway had been used to transport workers to and from the site, the LCC did not obtain any passenger carriages and no passengers were carried, though it is likely that some were occasionally given a ride on the line.

In 1935 the LCC purchased "Hendon", an 0-6-0 saddle tank engine, from a contractor and the old "Crossness" was cut up on site. During the Second World War, the hospital site was used as part of the air defences for London. Anti Aircraft guns were sited by the railway, which drew it unwelcome attention and it was bombed with some near misses for both the railway and the hospitals. Horton Hospital was again converted into a military hospital and did not return to its former use until 1949. During both military campaigns the hospital became a research centre for malaria and during the Second World War it led the world in developing treatment for the disease.

After the War in 1946 "Hendon" was sold and replaced with a new 0-4-0 locomotive "Sherwood" (also given the number 1). However, the life of the line was to be limited. The complex of hospitals was incorporated into the NHS in 1949 and the South West Regional Hospital Board decided that the railway should close in 1950. The rolling stock (the locomotive "Sherwood" and two ash wagons) were sold to Fred Watkins (Boilers) Ltd. and the rails went to scrap.

In 1973 Epsom and Ewell Borough Council purchased 400 acres of land that had formally been the farmland of the hospital complex. The Council founded Horton Country Park for the benefit of all.

Long Grove Hospital was closed in 1992 and has been demolished, the area now being a housing estate and Manor Hospital has gone the same way. Horton and West Park Hospitals have been closed and are in the process of being sold for development. St Ebba's is the subject of consultation on its future, but it is likely to have the same fate as the other hospitals in the group.

In the early days Ewell had two stations both with the same name, one owned by the LBSCR and the other by the LSWR. The LSWR station was later named Ewell West. Here is an early photograph.

# HASLAR ROYAL NAVY HOSPITAL

*Also known as:*
**Royal Hospital Haslar**

The history of medical care in the Royal Navy started in the 1400s with the appointment of sea-surgeons to Tudor warships. The first land based hospital, the Royal Hospital for injured seamen, was founded in Greenwich in 1694. In Gosport, opposite Portsmouth Harbour, the navy purchased Haslar Farm in 1745. Haslar Hospital was built on the site and it opened in 1753 with large buildings situated around a central quadrangle. It could accommodate up to 2,000 patients. At the time it was the largest brick building in Europe. One unusual hazard for the builders was the risk of being press-ganged to join the navy. Indeed the Admiralty had to issue an order protecting the workers on the building. Even this was not always effective. One worker had to be brought back from a Man O'War, saved because he had the cellar keys in his pocket!

Patients were brought to the hospital by ship or rowing boat to the jetty. From there they were taken to the hospital buildings by cart. In 1877 a 400-yard standard gauge tramway was built to provide a smoother journey from the jetty. The single tramcar carried seriously ill patients and it was powered by naval person-

**Clearly the passengers are not patients, but senior naval officers.**

**Inside the hospital there are still remnants of the tram rails. The patients would be taken off the trams protected from the elements for admission to the wards.**

**Looking along the tramway showing the standard gauge line to the hospital and the narrow gauge line turning left to run outside the hospital wall to the Zymotic Hospital.**

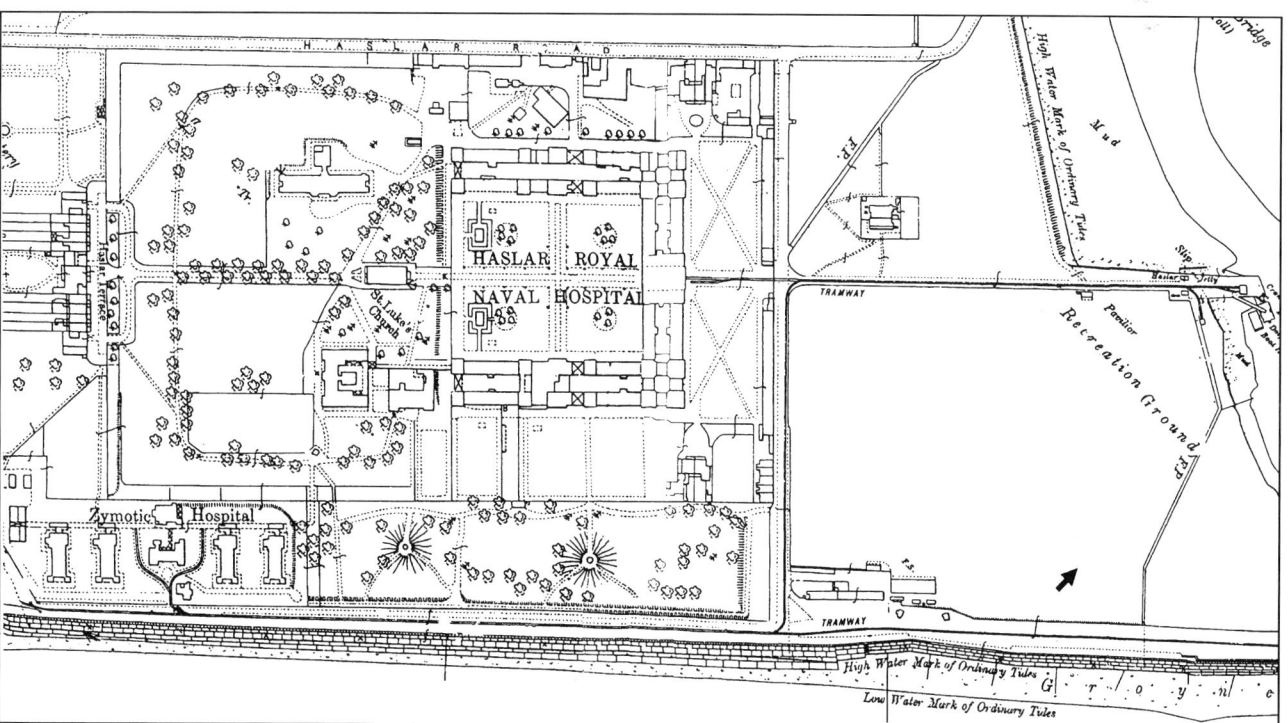
**Haslar Royal Navy Hospital showing the standard gauge passenger tramway from the jetty to the hospital and the 18-inch gauge goods tramway from the jetty to the Zymotic Hospital. Ordnance Survey 1910.**

The tramway was also used to carry dignitaries during official visits. The tramcar looks highly polished, possibly recently painted.

nel pushing it. It was also used to convey important senior officers and dignitaries visiting the hospital. In addition there was a one and a quarter miles, eighteen inch gauge, goods tramway. This took ammunition and stores between Fort Blockhouse, Fort Monkton and the Zymotic Wing (infectious diseases) of the hospital. Part of this ran along the same route of the passenger tramway on dual gauge track. The tramways were removed after 1918.

In the late 1990s, following the changes in the management of NHS care, the hospital became part of the NHS and cares for patients both military and civilian. It now has 112 beds. In 2003 the Hospital celebrated its 250th Anniversary.

**Now we know how many sailors it takes to move a tramcar. Rather a lot!**

# HELLINGLY HOSPITAL

*Also known as:*
**East Sussex County Asylum**
**East Sussex Mental Hospital**

Hellingly is a small community some eight miles north of Eastbourne. In 1897 the East Sussex County Council purchased 400 acres of woodland at Park Farm near Hellingly in order to build the new County Asylum. When the contract to build the Asylum was given it included a requirement for a tramway connecting the site with the London, Brighton and South Coast Railway (LBSCR) line at Hellingly station. Once the Hospital was built the line was to be left in good working order.

The tramway was built to standard gauge and the Council Visiting Committee paid the LBSCR £1,000 to build and maintain sidings at Hellingly Station for use by the hospital. The line was built as a single track route and the contractors used an 0-4-0 saddle tank to transport the materials for the building work.

Once the hospital was complete the locomotive was sold, while the hospital management decided that the line should be electrified, using power from the hospital's own generators. The line was equipped with overhead poles and wire

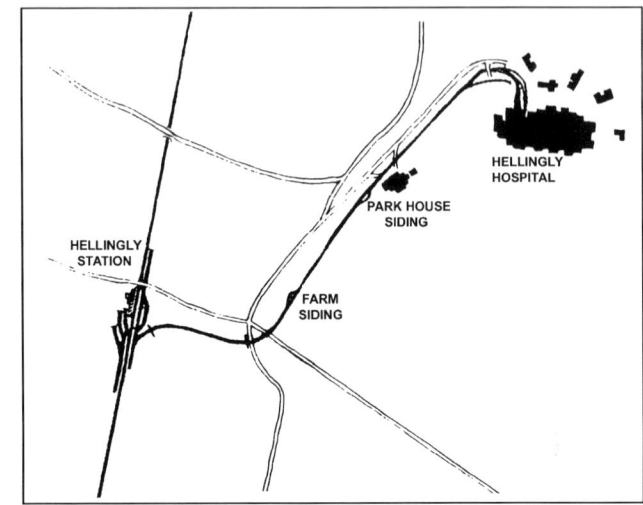
The Hellingly Hospital tramway.

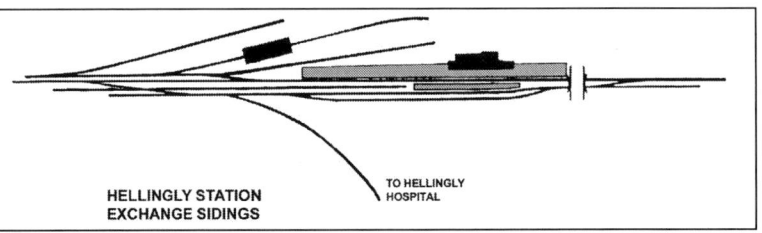

14

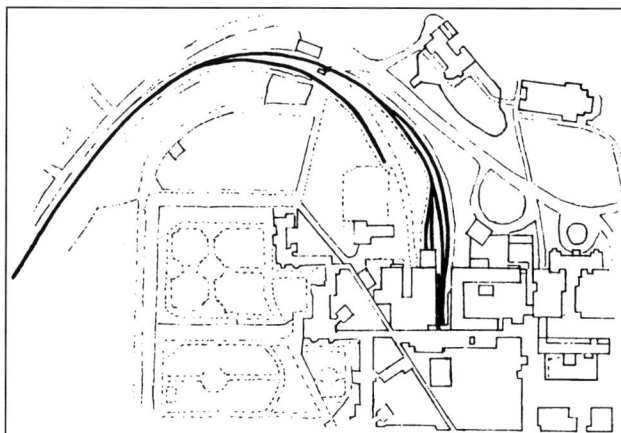
**Track layout by the hospital buildings.**

**The total powered fleet of the hospital. The small passenger tramcar and the diminutive electric steeple cab locomotive.**

and a small 0-4-0 electric locomotive was purchased, along with a tiny passenger tramcar built by Brush, which could carry just 12 people. To accommodate the passengers a wooden island platform had to be built at Hellingly Station. As the station only had one platform, the new platform was also alongside the main line. So this side of the platform was chained off to prevent passengers getting on or off from the railway trains. They could only have access to the hospital tramcar. There were also two loops on the line, roughly one third and two thirds along the line. One was called Farm Siding and was used by wagons of manure for farm use. The other was Park House Siding and used for passengers and goods going to Park House.

**Coal traffic was the main reason for the line. This train of four wagons must have been near the limit for the locomotive.**

The tramway continued in operation, carrying both passengers and goods, mainly coal, through the change to the Southern Railway in 1924. But by 1931 the passenger traffic had diminished and the hospital managers decided to close the passenger service. The extra platform at Hellingly Station was removed in 1933 and the tramcar was taken off its chassis and used as a sports pavilion on the hospital sports ground. During the Second World War part of the hospital was used as a military hospital. The War Ministry investigated the possibility of operating trains over the tramway to carry wounded troops to the hospital. In the event Park House was used to treat Canadian Army patients and they were taken from Hellingly Station to the hospital by road. So the tramway remained a goods only line. However, in the early 1950s it became a popular place for railway enthusiasts to visit. A variety of railway societies chartered trips on the line, using a British Railways guards van as an impromptu passenger coach.

In line with the government's policy the hospital converted its boilers to oil firing in the 1950s and the requirement for coal ceased. So the tramway was closed. The last goods use was on 10 March 1959, though the Norbury Transport and Model Railway Club paid a visit on 4 April and were taken up and down the line in a guards van. The line,

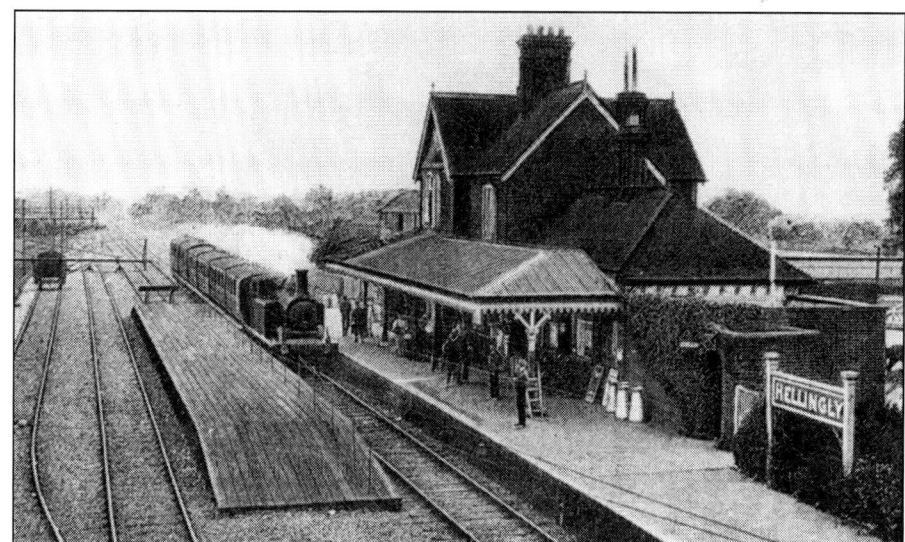
**Hellingly Station on the LBSCR. The hospital tramway is on the left. The wooden platform is for the tramcar. Note the railings on the right of that platform to prevent LBSCR passengers alighting that side. There seems to be no provision for passengers to get access to the wooden platform.**

**A very evocative photograph showing both trams and the competitor that would eventually force the closure of the line.**

overhead and locomotive were all sold for scrap. The hospital was closed in 1994 and has since stood derelict and has been targeted by arsonists.

The hospital tramway has also been the basis of a fine operating model railway layout. This recreates the atmosphere of the tramway in its early days and is a fine testament to this unusual line.

A superb model of Hellingly Hospital Tramway. The passenger tram is off to the station to collect visitors and staff.

The main workhorse of the tramway was this tiny steeple cab locomotive. It operated over the whole of the lifetime of the tramway.

# HIGH ROYDS HOSPITAL

*Also known as:*
**Menston Hospital**
**Menston Mental Hospital**
**West Riding County Lunatic Asylum**

In 1882 the West Riding of Yorkshire Asylum Committee recognised the pressures on existing mental health facilities. The following year they purchased 300 acres of land from Mr Ayscough Fawkes of Farnley Hall. The land was near Menston roughly seven miles north of Bradford. Over the next five years a large mental hospital was built, with room for 1,526 patients. During the building a half mile standard gauge tramway line was constructed to connect the hospital with the Otley and Ilkley Extension line of the Midland Railway south of Menston Station. During the construction the contractor used a steam locomotive. The hospital opened on 8 October 1888. The line continued to be operated by a small steam locomotive. The line had some very steep sections and the locomotive was not up to the job. In 1897 the line was electrified, with a tramway type overhead. An electric tramway locomotive was purchased that had a simple trolley type collector. This also proved to be underpowered and it was only able to haul one wagon at a time. The locomotive lasted until 1924 when a more powerful electric locomotive, built by English Electric, was purchased and the old engine scrapped.

The procedure was that the Midland Railway would deliver a train of wagons to the exchange sidings by the main line. Then the hospital locomotive would take the wagons one at a time to whichever part of the hospital was appropriate. Coal was taken to the boiler house on a short siding that was raised. This allowed the wagon doors to be opened and the coal fell out into hoppers, ready for feeding to the boilers. The boilers also powered a 110-volt DC generator for the tramway. Sacks of flour were unloaded by the bakery, goods delivered to the hospital and fertiliser and other farm supplies

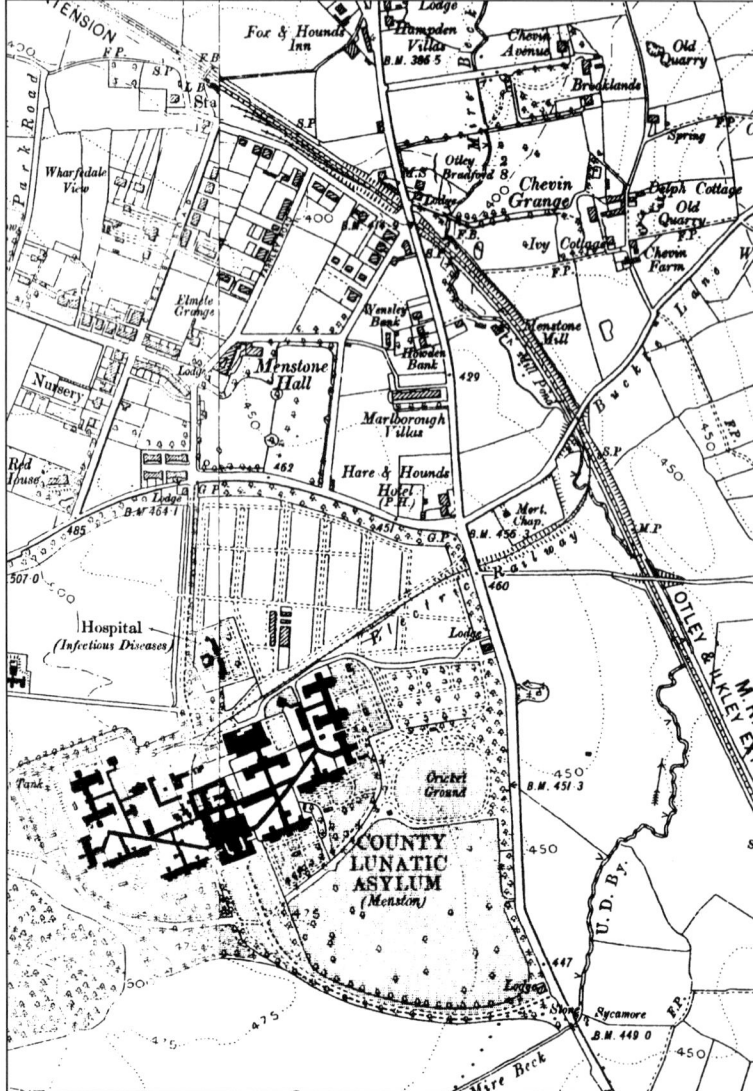

**High Royds Hospital Tramway** connects the hospital with the Midland Railway. Ordnance Survey 1909.

16

were taken to the hospital's large market gardens.

During the 1930s the Midland Railway approached the hospital stating that the sidings by the main line required repairs and this would cost the hospital over £400. The hospital responded by saying that most supplies were being delivered by road and the tramway was not needed. So they closed the line. A few years later war broke out and the Government asked that the line be re-opened to save petrol and diesel on the road vehicles delivering to the hospital. The hospital management agreed and the line was re-opened, though everyone stayed quiet about any repairs to the sidings. So the tramway gave service throughout the war. But during this time the line suffered from a lack of maintenance and it deteriorated further. After the war, as soon as road fuel became more available, the tramway was used less and less. In 1951 the decision was taken to close it and sell the equipment for scrap.

The hospital continued to serve the community until February 2003 when it was closed, with the mental health services being provided elsewhere. The empty hospital building was used in 2004 for the filming of Asylum, a romantic thriller set at a top security psychiatric asylum near London in 1959. The hospital site was sold to a property developer for £26 million and will be turned into a 500-home development over five years.

On the exchange sidings the steeple cab locomotive prepares to take a full coal wagon to the hospital.

A closer view of the steeple cab locomotive.

# HOLLYMOOR HOSPITAL

*Also known as:*
**City of Birmingham Lunatic Asylum**

The railway line to Hollymoor Hospital was unusual in being a line that was only used for the construction of the hospital. It was removed by the contractor once all building work was completed. In the late 1800s the City of Birmingham looked for land to the south of the city to build two large mental health hospitals. A large tract of land was purchased that was then outside the city boundary, in Worcestershire. It was just north of the road from Rubery to Longbridge. At that time the whole of the area was farm land. The land they purchased was bisected by the Halesowen Branch of the Midland and Great Western Joint Railway (M&GWJR). The city decided to build one hospital to the west of the railway, Rubery and this was opened in 1882. A second hospital, Hollymoor, was then built to the east of the railway. Construction started in 1900, the contract for building Hollymoor having been given to John Bowen and Sons. The contractor arranged with the M&GWJR for a branch to be built from Rubery Station to the hospital site. The line ran parallel to the branch line from Rubery Station before turning northwards and running close to Tessall Lane. At the building site there was a loop to allow the engine to be run around the wagons. The contractor purchased a new locomotive for the project and this

Most of the Hollymoor Hospital has been demolished, but some buildings remain, like the water tower.

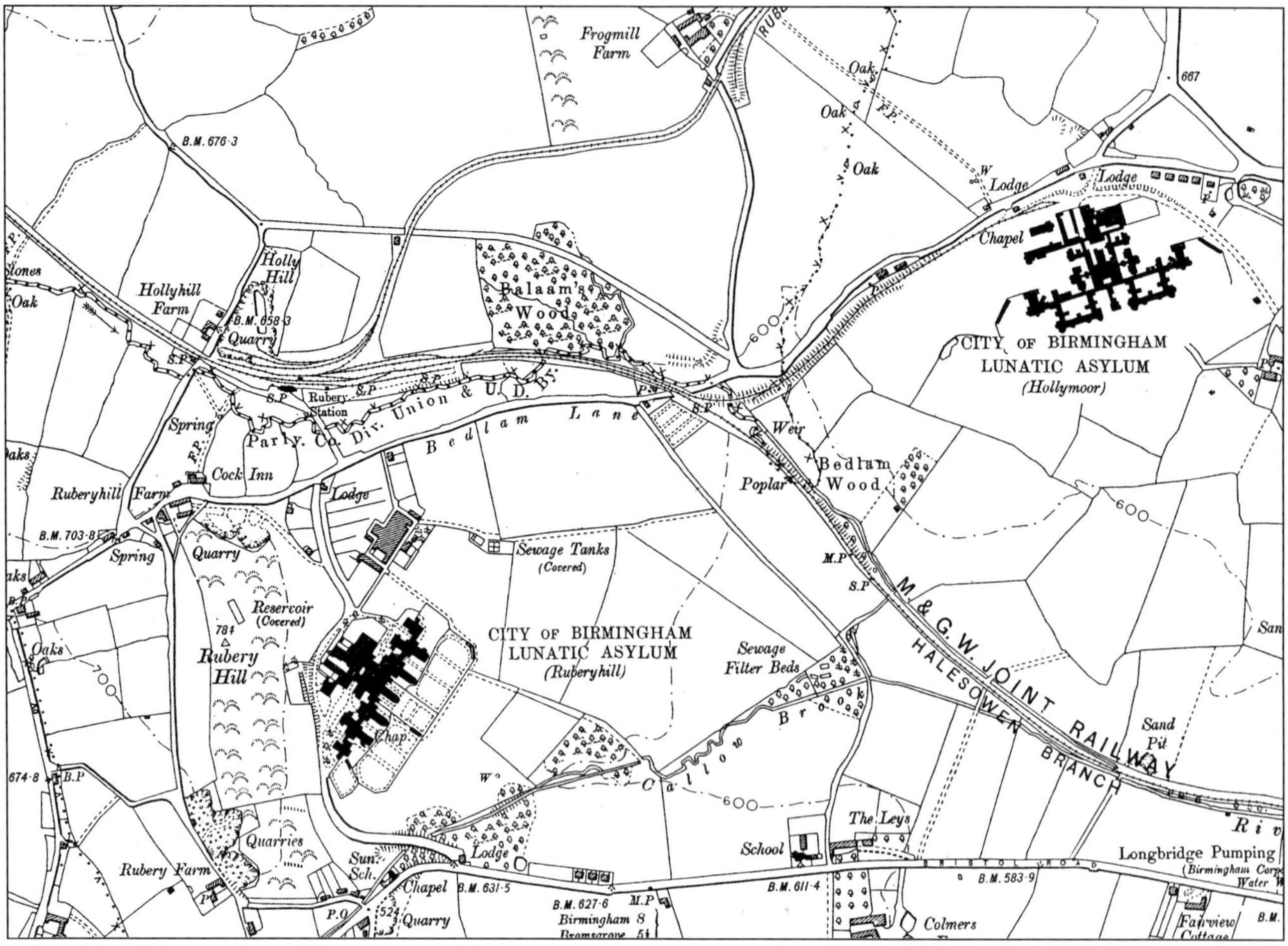

**Although the Hollymoor Hospital Railway only lasted a couple of years, it coincided with an Ordnance Survey review and it appears on the 1904 edition of the OS map.**

was sold when the building work was close to completion in 1904. The railway was used for taking building materials directly to the building site. It may also have been used to carry workers from the station to the building site, though there is no record of any carriages being used.

It is unusual that the hospital management decided not to take on the line once the hospital was complete. The hospital closed in 1994 and most of the buildings were demolished and the site is now a housing estate.

**I have not been able to find any photograph of the contractor's railway. This shows Rubery Station where the line to the hospital began. In the foreground is a quarry railway that is similar to the contractor's railway.**

**The church is another building that has been preserved.**

# JOYCE GREEN HOSPITAL

*Incorporating:*
**Long Reach Hospital**
**Orchard Hospital**

In the late 1800s in London the Metropolitan Asylums Board was responsible for providing hospitals for infectious diseases as well as for the mentally ill. In 1867 they had commissioned hospitals that opened in 1870. This was fortuitous as a smallpox epidemic began soon after the hospitals were opened. But because the hospitals were in highly populated parts of the city there were many complaints, leading to a Royal Commission. This determined that smallpox should be treated in ships or hospitals situated in isolated parts of the banks of the Thames. Several fever hulks were taken on. By 1894 this arrangement was no longer satisfactory so the Board purchased farm land on the Dartford Marshes. After a delay an infrastructure of a pier, roads and a four-foot gauge horse tramway

An early photograph of the tramway, showing staff in their period uniforms. This could be at the opening of the hospital.

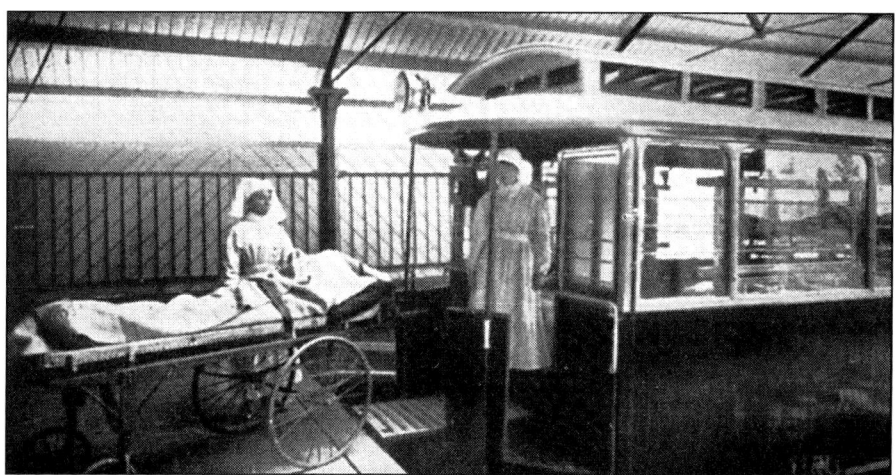
Inside the transfer shed on the jetty, showing how the stretcher is moved from the trolley to the tramcar.

For such a small tramway it had a remarkably large fleet of trams. This shows them all lined up outside the tram shed. The trams were made in two sizes, the larger one requiring two horses to power it.

One of the trams in use. The back ramp is down and the patient is being carried into the ward by two orderlies. This photograph is in the later life the tramway, when motor ambulances were used to haul the tramcars.

When the proposal to electrify the tramway was rejected on cost grounds, the horses were replaced with motor ambulances. They continued to the close of the tramway.

A rather poor photograph but it is included because of its interest. It shows the inside of one of the larger tramcars, with four fold down beds.

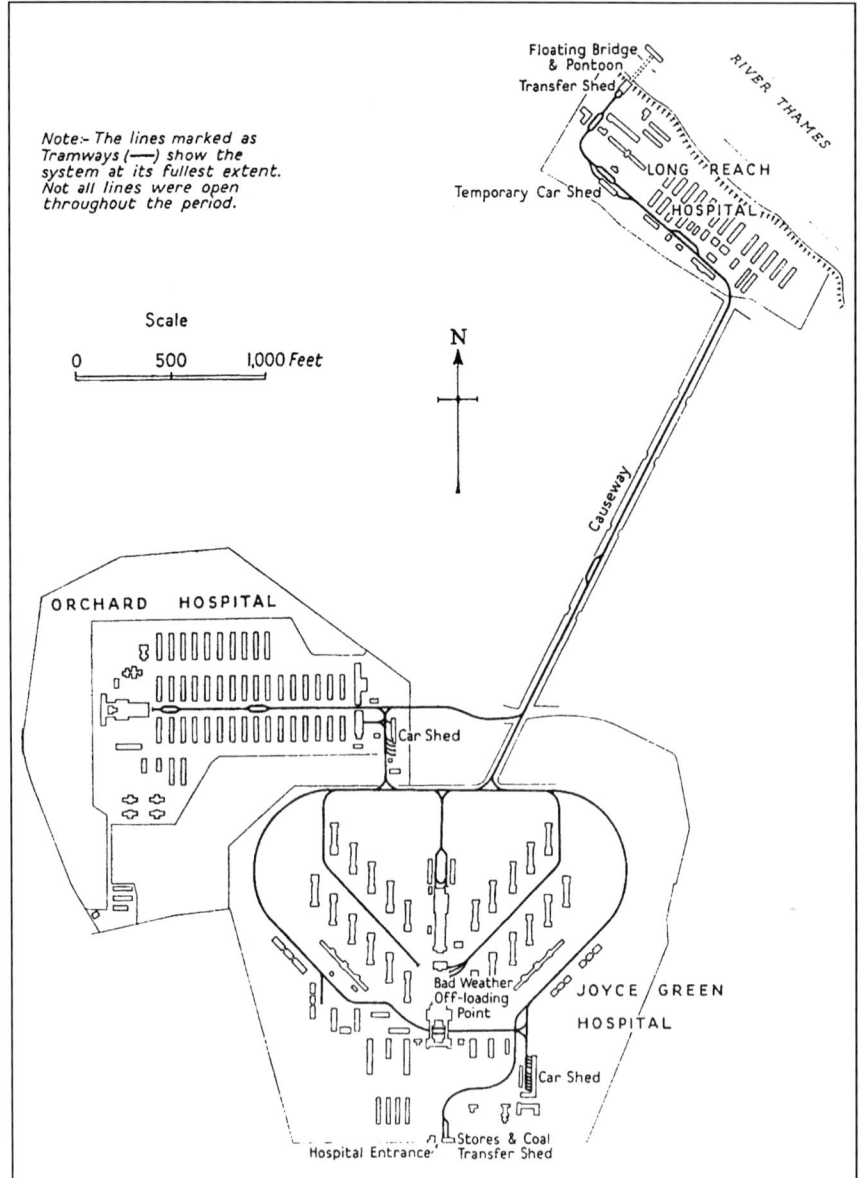

The tramway at Joyce Green Hospital was the last horse tramway to run in London. Map F. Merton Atkins courtesy Tramway and Light Railway Society.

# KNOWLE HOSPITAL

*Also known as:*
**Hampshire County Lunatic Asylum**
**Hampshire County Mental Hospital**
**Knowle Mental Hospital**

In 1851 Hampshire County proposed a large mental hospital and they purchased the 105-acre farm known as Knowle Farm for £5,550. This was located half way between Fareham and Wickham. It was a very isolated rural location, but it was very close to the London and South Western Railway's main line between London and Portsmouth. Advantage was taken of this and a platform halt was built on the line for staff and visitors. A little further

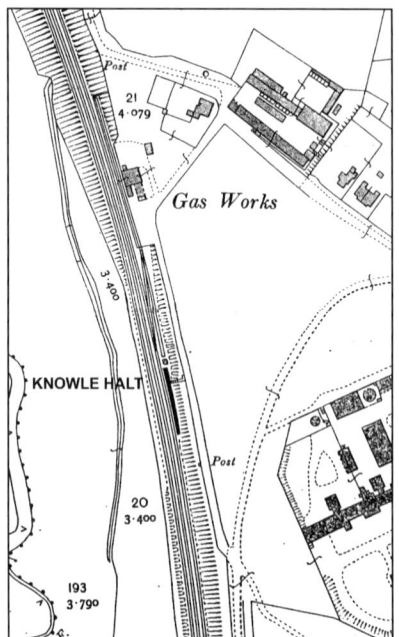

**Detail showing the Halt and hospital siding.**

**Knowle Halt in 1963, a year before the halt closed. The photograph shows Ralph Ford and his son Gary.**

was constructed in 1897. This was to take patients relatively smoothly from the ships at the pier to the hospital wards. Given the level of road vehicle technology at that time, the patients would have been grateful not to have to ride in a road ambulance. A sudden outbreak of smallpox meant that a temporary hutted hospital was built beside the river, and a second larger temporary hospital at the Orchard. Four second-hand horse trams were used. A permanent hospital at Joyce Green was opened in 1903. After considering getting more second-hand tramcars the Board decided to have five trams purpose built for the hospital complex. As the incidence of smallpox declined Joyce Green and Orchard Hospitals were re-designated as infectious diseases hospitals, leaving just Long Reach Hospital dedicated to smallpox. During the First World War Orchard Hospital was requisitioned by the War Office, where it was used to treat Australian troops.

The idea of converting the tramway to electric power, or using petrol locomotives was explored on several occasions, but the cost proved too much. Then in 1925 they carried out some trials by towing the trams with petrol ambulances. These proved successful and horse power ceased. In 1930 the London County Council took over management of the hospitals. They decided that their large fleet of ambulances could handle patient movement and the decision was taken to bring in all patients by road. Use of the tramway declined completely and it was formally closed in 1938 when the tramcars were sold. The rails were lifted in 1943 as part of the war effort.

From around the 1960s Orchard and Long Reach Hospitals were closed and Joyce Green became a General Hospital. Then in 2000 Darent Valley Hospital was opened in Dartford and it took the work from three old hospitals including Joyce Green. The site was sold and is now to become a major shopping, housing, business park and recreational area.

This was the main entrance to Knowle hospital. It has been preserved as a part of the residential development and is now a block of apartments.

north a private siding was built to take wagons of coal for the boiler house. The maps of the time are slightly misleading as they indicate the sidings to be serving the Gas Works. This was an acetylene production plant and did not require any coal. The coal from the wagons was distributed by lorry to the staff homes and the boiler house.

The hospital opened in November 1852, initially accommodated 600 patients, but soon increased to over 1,000 by 1883. During this year the hospital buildings were extended using Russian prisoners from the Crimean War. In 1915 the hospital had to take more patients to free up the West Sussex Asylum for the treatment of wounded troops. Things went back to normal in 1919. During the Second World War part of the hospital was taken over by Haslar Royal Navy Hospital as its psychiatric annexe. The hospital was also subject to bombing raids, one of which caused damage to several buildings, killing a sailor. In 1958 the boilers were converted to oil firing, thus eliminating the need for the coal delivery.

The platform was originally known as Knowle Asylum Halt; however, the name was changed in 1942 to Knowle Halt. Though no express trains ever stopped at the Halt, there were six local trains a day plus the goods trains taking wagons to and from the sidings. It has been reported as a very busy place on visiting days. Following a lack of traffic the Halt closed in 1964. The sidings became disused around the same time, though they remained intact for several years.

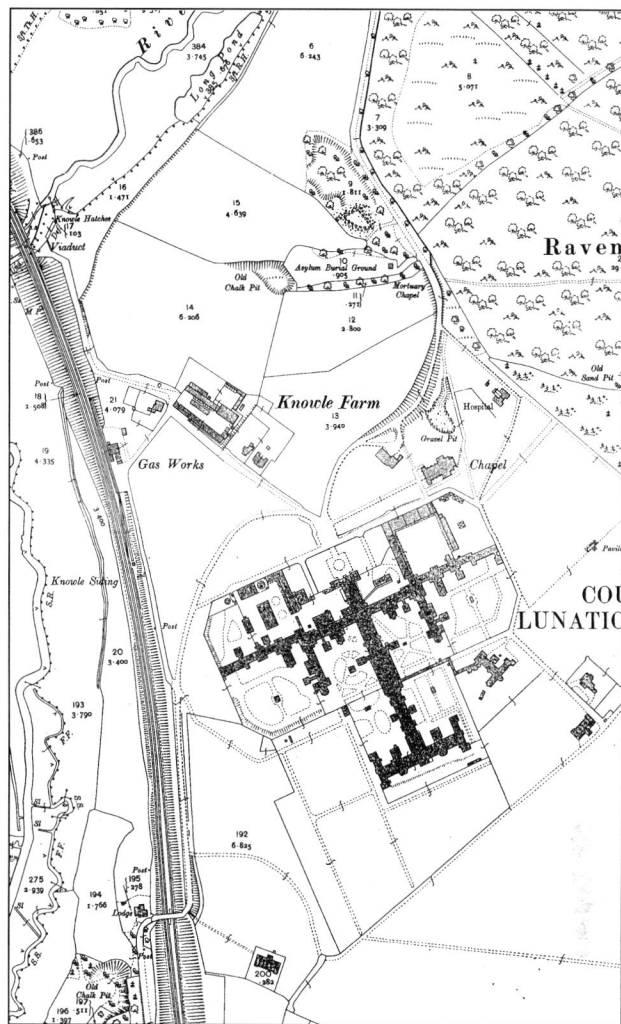

Knowle Hospital and the railway. Ordnance Survey map 1909.

The hospital closed in 1996 and the site was sold for the development of housing. Now known as Knowle Village, the site has around 500 dwellings. Some of the original hospital buildings have been kept and renovated and converted to apartment blocks. The church was also refurbished and survives.

Knowle Halt was a very Spartan station. Note the stairs behind the shelter lead to the hospital.

# LORD MAYOR TRELOAR'S HOSPITAL

*Also known as:*
   **Lord Mayor Treloar's Cripples Home and College**
   **Lord Mayor Treloar's Cripples Hospital and College**
   **Lord Mayor Treloar's Hospital and College**
   **Treloar's Hospital**
   **Alton Park**
   **Cripples Home Siding**

Originally named Lord Mayor Treloar's Cripples Home and College (later Lord Mayor Treloar's Cripples Hospital and College and finally dropping the word Cripples to become Lord Mayor Treloar's Hospital and College), the hospital was opened in 1908, but the history of its railway goes further back than that. The site of the hospital was 2½ kilometres south west of Alton in Hampshire. It had originally been built as an A.M.B. (Armoured Motor Battery) Hospital to provide convalescent healthcare to soldiers wounded in the 1899-1902 Boer War. The accommodation was spread out in single storey huts. Following the end of the war the hospital came to the end of its useful life and was abandoned.

In 1897 the London and South Western Railway obtained a Light Railway Order to build a line between Basingstoke and Alton. Opened to passengers on 1 June 1901 the line ran alongside the A.M.B. Hospital as it turned to connect with the Mid Hampshire line at Butts Junction, by Alton. In a description of the first passenger journey the A.M.B. hospital was described as having "a very absent minded appearance", so was presumably much run down at the time, though still open. There is a hint that the railway connection to the hospital was part of the original line, the connection being severed when the hospital was closed.

In 1907 the Lord Mayor of London, Sir William Treloar, had become concerned about the plight of crippled children in London. He decided to build a hospital in the country for children suffering from non-pulmonary tuberculosis. The aim of the hospital was "to train and educate boys and girls to face the battle of life with confidence and courage". He established his Little Cripples Fund and made appeals to the public for donations. Sufficient money was raised by 1908 to convert the old A.M.B. hospital near Alton into a hospital for the children where they could benefit from the fresh air and sunshine of the countryside. To coincide with the opening of the hospital a platform was built on the Basingstoke to Alton branch line and either the existing siding re-connected or a new siding laid to take coal wagons to the boiler house. On the railway diagrams this was known as "Cripples Siding", a name unlikely to be used today!

The platform was called "Alton Park" and carried the name "Alton Park – Lord Treloar Cripples Home and College – supported by voluntary contributions. – London Offices Moorgate House". Just past the platform a point led to a stub siding with a reversed point taking the line to the boiler house, with a truck turntable. The siding was used solely to take coal to the boiler house, needing around 1,500 tons a year. Locomotives were not allowed on the rails within the hospital grounds so would shunt trucks into the stub siding and leave them there. The trucks would then be run down the gradient to the boiler house. To remove them a power winch was set up by the stub siding to allow the empty trucks to be hauled by cable out of the hospital grounds and ready to be picked up by a locomotive. Passengers were carried to Alton Park Halt, but only on Thursdays when two trains during the day would stop there. In addition, once a year a Founder's Day special train would travel from London taking dignitaries and visitors to the Hospital. These continued until the start of the Second World War.

The hospital was very successful in treating the children and it expanded to take in adults as an orthopaedic hospital. Along with most other hospitals it became part of the NHS in 1948.

In 1916 the Government needed railway lines for the war effort in France. They asked the railway companies to contribute second-hand track or to shut lines and lift the track to take to France. The contribution from the London and South Western Railway was set at twelve miles. This was just the length of the Basingstoke to Alton branch. The Company took advantage of this to close what had become a very uneconomic line. So the rails were lifted, leaving only access to the Thornycroft Factory near Basingstoke and the Lord Mayor Treloar's Hospital near Alton. This was accepted by the local population as their contri-

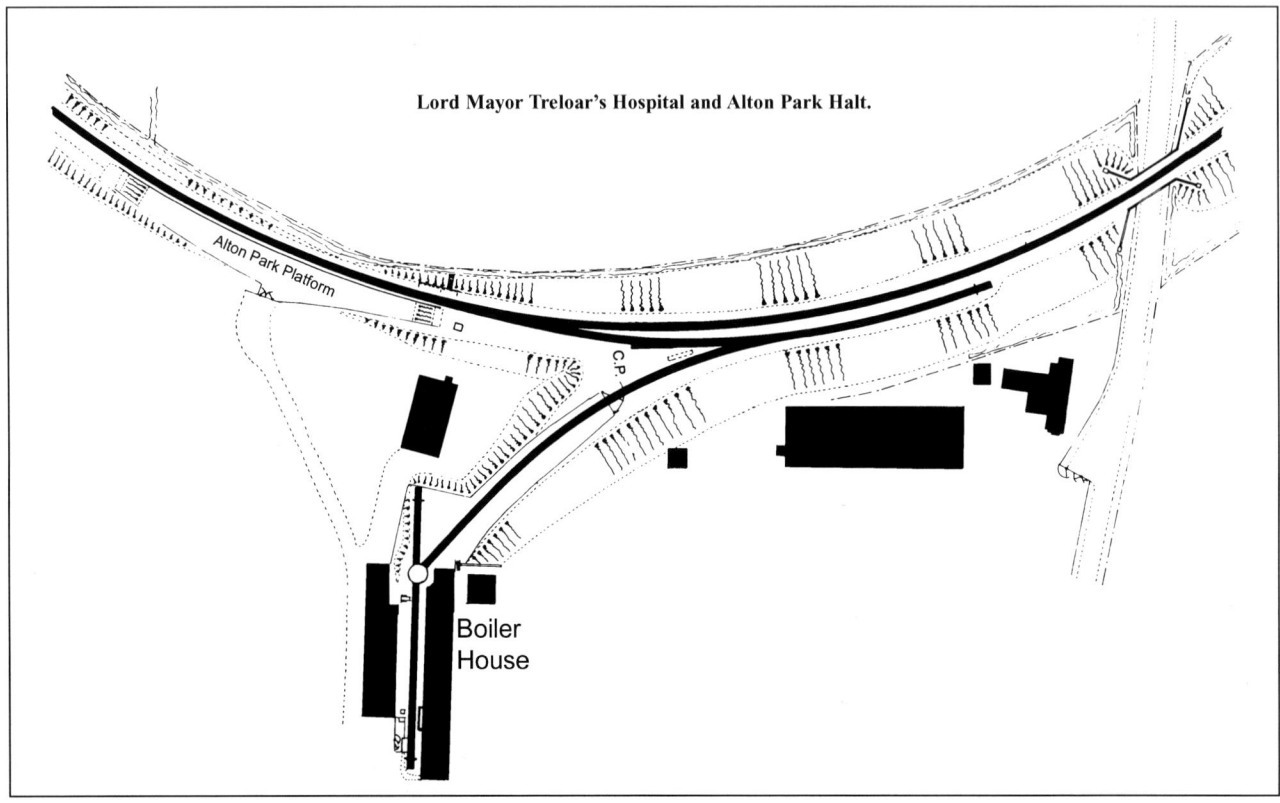

Lord Mayor Treloar's Hospital and Alton Park Halt.

bution to the war effort. They expected the line to be re-opened after the war. However, in 1922 the LSWR applied for authority to formally close the line that had not operated for six years. This produced a reaction in the local population who opposed the application. By now the LSWR was part of the Southern Railway which was still sorting its management structure. They lost their application due to the local pressure and the line was rebuilt and re-opened to passengers on 18 August 1924.

However, the extended life of the branch line was to be fairly short. The line continued to lose money and it was closed to passenger operation in 1932 and goods operation in 1936. Track lifting began in 1937, but the goods services to Thornycrofts and Lord Mayor Treloar's Hospital continued.

The line gained some publicity on two occasions. In 1928 Gainsborough Pictures Ltd arranged with the Southern Railway to use part of the line, by Salter Hatch Crossing, to film a spectacular railway crash. The company had purchased a locomotive and six carriages and ran them into a Foden Steam lorry on the crossing. This was for the film "The Wrecker". After filming the debris was cleared and the line went back to normal operation. Then in 1937, after some of the line had been removed, the same film company hired Cliddesden Station for the filming of the Will Hay classic comedy "Oh! Mr Porter". The station became "Buggleskelly" and three old locomotives were used. When the filming was completed track removal continued and the branch line finally ceased all hope of further operation. Track was lifted, but leaving access to the hospital siding.

The line to Lord Mayor Treloar's Hospital continued to operate, taking coal to the boiler house, but after the war the only passengers to ride to Alton Park Halt were specials organised by the Railway Enthusiasts Club of Farnborough and a few Founder's Day specials. The last railway enthusiast's trip was on 15 October 1960 and it was the last journey for passengers. The coal trains to Treloar's Hospital ceased on 11 July 1967 and the hospital railway closed and most of the track was lifted. The Hospital itself closed in 1995 and the land was sold to a property developer in 2001. An estate of 183 homes has been built, with plans for a further 150 homes and some business premises. In 2004 the Office of the Deputy Prime Minister purchased the site back for the government in order to encourage affordable housing for local people. Part of the railway still existed in the late 1990s with the first part of the track from the main line to the hospital still in place, over 30 years since the last train travelled on it.

An early view of Alton Park Halt, with a wooden platform and the early sign. The children are identified by the labels pinned on their coats.

Alton Park Halt in later days with a concrete surface. By the signal is the point leading to the hospital sidings.

The line to the left runs into the hospital grounds, while Alton Park Halt is in the background to the right. Note the capstan on the left of the point, used to winch wagons from the hospital.

# NETLEY MILITARY HOSPITAL

*Also known as:*
**Royal Victoria Military Hospital**

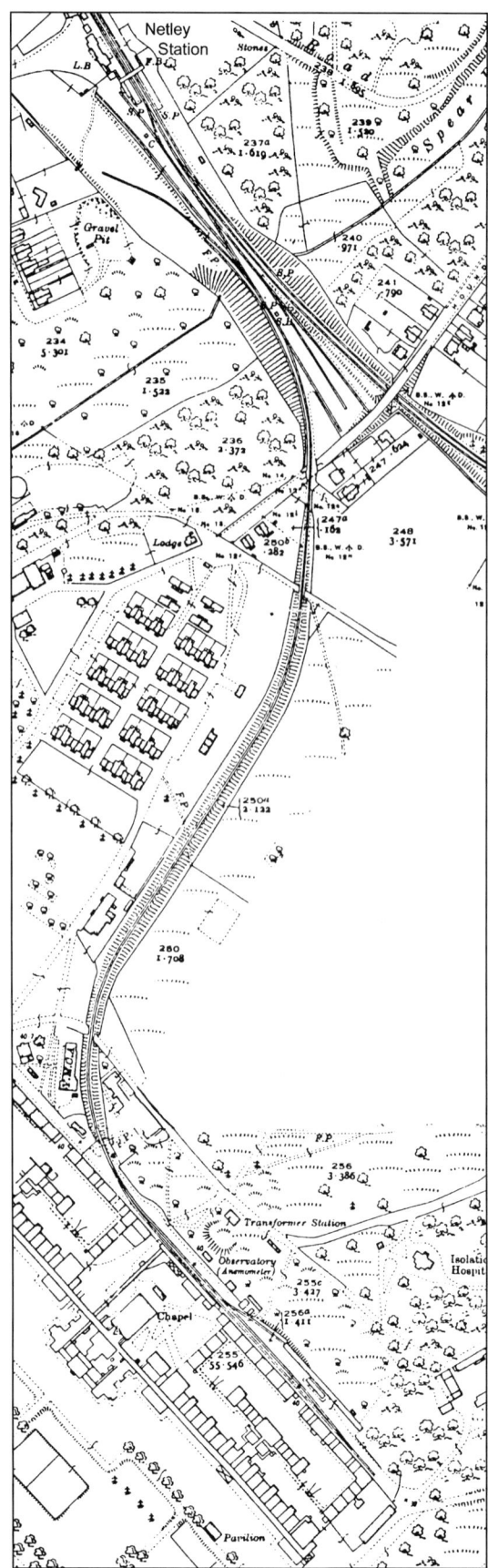

Netley Hospital Railway from Netley Station to the Royal Victoria Hospital.

During the Crimean War messages got back to Britain giving disturbing reports of heavy casualties and dreadful conditions in the military hospitals. This directly led to Florence Nightingale going to the Crimea with other nurses to improve care for the casualties. Large numbers of wounded were coming back to this country and hospital accommodation was needed. So the government set about looking for a suitable site for a 1,000-bedded hospital. One of the criteria was that it should be accessible from the sea to minimise travelling for soldiers. A logical place was near the large naval bases at Portsmouth or Plymouth. A site was selected on the coast east of Southampton at Netley Grange Farm and eventually around 200 acres were purchased. In order to take the number of patients envisaged a building a quarter of a mile long on three storeys was designed. Queen Victoria laid the foundation stone in 1856 and gave her name to the hospital. Under the stone there was a casket containing the first Victoria Cross, a silver Crimea medal and some coins. The hospital opened in 1863 having cost £350,000, to immediate criticism from Florence Nightingale, who felt that the design of the buildings did not give sufficient ventilation and fresh air, and she was also concerned at its poor accessibility. Indeed the plans were that patients would arrive by water on to a 500-foot long pier.

The London and South Western Railway (LSWR) started planning a rail link once it was known that the hospital was to be built at Netley. In 1863 work started on building a railway between Southampton and Netley. It opened in 1866, three years after the hospital accepted its first patients, however, the railway stopped at Netley and did not extend into the hospital grounds. In 1889 an extension from Netley to connect with the main line at Fareham opened. It was a single line leading to a terminal with a loop siding and a single platform. The extension to the hospital itself

The platform at the hospital with plenty of servicemen waiting for their train. Railway workers maintain the track.

Looking along the track as an ambulance train arrives at Netley Hospital.

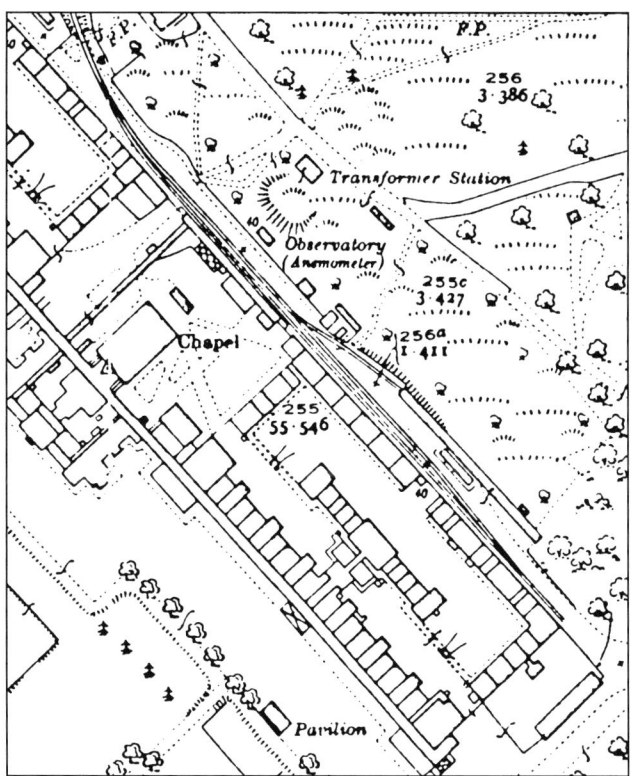
Detail of the track layout in the grounds of Netley Hospital. Ordnance Survey 1933.

An ambulance train in the hospital station during the First World War.

opened some time later in 1900. Now that a rail link to the hospital itself had been established the use of the pier diminished. This coincided with the start of the Boer War. Such was the demand for the services of the hospital additional huts had to be built and the number of beds doubled to 2,000.

The line from Southampton to Netley and Fareham was made double track in 1910-11. This was another fortunate event as a few years later the First World War began and the hospital and railway had their biggest test. Between 1914 and 1918 around 1,000 hospital trains ran between Southampton and Netley taking 50,000 patients for treatment at the hospital.

Netley had a quiet inter-war period. At the start of the Second World War there was a slow build up of patients, increasing greatly as the Dunkirk evacuation took place. The next very busy time came in preparation for D-Day. In 1944 most of the hospital was handed over to the American Army. The US Army had taken British coaches and converted them into hospital trains with bunks three high lined up in the coaches. Each train consisted of 14 such coaches. They were needed as 68,000 patients were treated over an eighteen month period. Once the initial invasion had been completed the number of patients arriving at the hospital had fallen to the pre-D-Day levels. Indeed after the war there were very few trains going to the hospital, roughly one a year up to 1955. This was the year that saw the last train to the hospital. The cost of running the hospital was very high and not economic for the level of demand placed on it. So in 1958 the main hospital was closed, leaving just the psychiatric hospital still operative.

In 1963 there was a major fire in the main hospital building, which is believed to have been started by vandals. This led to its demolition, with the railway station in 1967.

A view from Netley Station with the main line for Fareham going to the left and the hospital line to the right.

However, the railway track itself remained in place until 1978, though totally unusable. This was the year that the psychiatric hospital was closed and the following year Hampshire County Council purchased the grounds and buildings to turn it into a park. The Royal Victoria Country Park opened to the public in 1980. Only two of the original buildings remain; the Royal Chapel and the Officer's Mess, now converted into luxury apartments.

The building on the left is the carriage shed where ambulance trains were stored.

25

# PARK PREWETT HOSPITAL

*Also known as:*
**Park Prewett Mental Hospital**

Hampshire County Council built Knowle hospital in 1852 to treat the mentally ill patients in their county. However, it soon became apparent that demand was going to outstrip the facilities. In 1898 the County Council appointed a special committee to investigate the feasibility of building a new asylum. The committee reported that there was a need for such a hospital and that it should be built in the north of the county, near Basingstoke. The hospital should have special access to railway facilities to make travel for patients and visitors as convenient as possible. They narrowed the choice to either Winkleberry Farm or Park Prewett Farm. The Council decided to buy Park Prewett Farm that was a few miles west of Basingstoke. The Council bought 300 acres of land at a cost of £30 per acre. Apparently the farm came complete with a resident ghost. In 1899 architects were appointed.

However, in 1902 the arrangement by which Bournemouth and Southampton patients were treated at Knowle ceased and they went to alternative hospitals. This relieved the pressure on Knowle and in 1905 it had 70 empty beds. This arrangement was reversed in 1908 and the Bournemouth and Southampton patients returned to Knowle Hospital, so the Council felt it necessary to resurrect the new hospital at Park Prewett. They reached an agreement with the two cities and of the 1300 beds 175 were financed by Bournemouth, 500 by Southampton and 625 by Hampshire County Council. A contract for the building was given in 1913 at a cost of £258,777. In addition to the hospital accommodating the patients the building work included cottages for staff. At the same time extra land for the railway line to the hospital was purchased at a cost of £700.

When work started there were over 300 men on the site. An

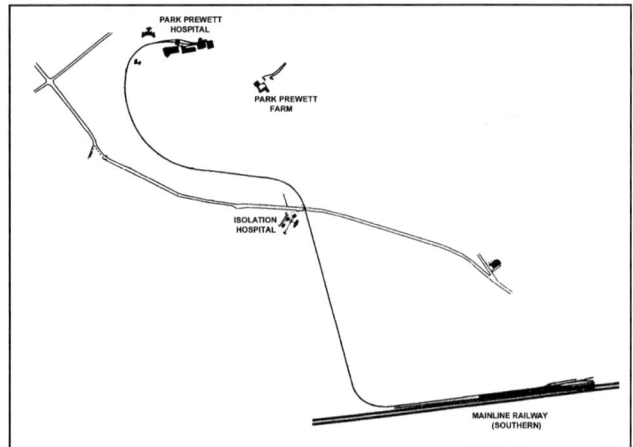

**The railway line to Park Prewett Hospital, also known as the long siding. The tight curves are evident.**

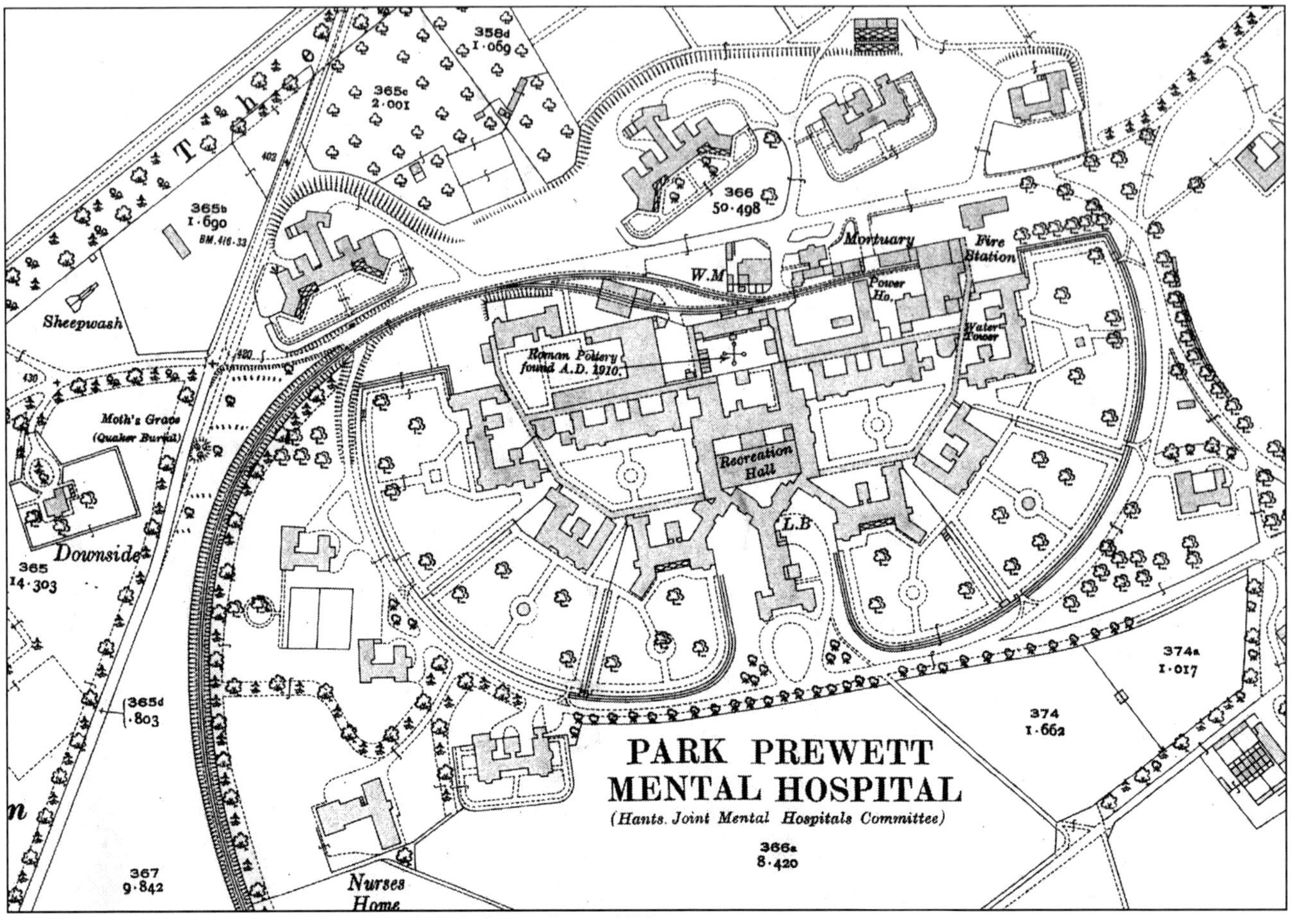

application was made to the London and South Western Railway (LSWR) to connect to the LSWR main line west of Basingstoke. This was agreed and the hospital railway was quickly built and used to transport the building materials to the site. The line itself had several sharp curves and a steep 1 in 53 gradient up to the hospital. Indeed all trains were pushed up the incline to the hospital to ensure that the wagons could never runaway (a runaway wagon could have led to a crash on the main line with serious consequences).

The outbreak of the First World War meant a loss of manpower and in 1915 work had to cease. However, the government decided that they needed the hospital for army use. So it was given a high priority and work started again. The main asylum was to be set up as a 200-bed military hospital. It was

**Detail of the track layout in Park Prewett Hospital. Ordnance Survey 1933.**

26

completed in 1917 as a 150-bedded unit under the control of the Canadian Army. Its name was Number Four Canadian General Hospital. The Canadians stayed in residence for two years. During this time the railway was used to carry goods, mainly coal to the boiler house. There is no record of it being used for passengers, despite the original recommendation of the advisory committee.

In 1919 the Canadian Army moved out and the hospital was emptied. The equipment, furniture and bedding were all auctioned off. The County Council saw an opportunity and were able to purchase most of it at a knock down price. The name of the hospital became Park Prewitt Mental Hospital. The Council purchased a further 226 acres of farmland and built 20 staff cottages. The Council had a shock in 1920 when the Ministry of Pensions approached them with a view to taking over the hospital for use by military pensioners. But they then changed their minds and the Council was able to go ahead with their plans. The first patient was admitted in August 1921. The railway continued to carry goods to the hospital. Although the railway was a private line, there was an arrangement with the LSWR (later the Southern Railway) that they would provide the locomotive power and rolling stock and actually run the line. So trains would arrive at the siding and haul trucks to the hospital. On one occasion a driver new to the line did not realise that coal trucks were fly shunted to the coal store. He pushed them all the way only to find that his engine hit the roof of the building bringing it down. At times when there was no engine at the hospital the wagons would be manhandled around the siding.

During the Second World War the hospital was requisitioned by the War Office and the resident patients were relocated to other mental hospitals. Park Prewett became a 2,000 bedded Emergency Medical Service General Hospital. As there was a railway to the hospital building the War Office carried out a trial to see if hospital trains could be run right up to the hospital

**Aerial view of Park Prewett Hospital with the railway just visible on the right.**

buildings. A train of eight bogie carriages with an engine at each end was taken along the line. Difficulty was experienced getting the coaches around the tight curves. When the train was taken back one of the carriages overhung the line so much that it dug into the embankment and the crew had a hard time getting the train back to the main line. The experience was such that the idea of using it for hospital trains was abandoned. This is the only recorded time that any passenger vehicles used the line. The goods traffic continued and some trains were so heavy that they required a locomotive at each end.

The hospital reverted to its former function after the war. Like many other hospitals the main stay of the line, coal, started to be delivered by road, because it was cheaper. The line continued to be used for other goods with about 100 tons of materials being moved each week. The track had deteriorated badly and by 1948 very little traffic, if any, used the branch line. Matters came to a head in 1950 when British Railway approached the Hospital Management Committee requiring that the track be repaired at an estimated cost of £18,000. They found it less expensive to arrange for the remaining goods to be delivered by road and so the line fell into disuse. So it was decided that the line should be closed in 1954, the track being lifted for scrap in 1956.

The hospital was closed in 1996 and the grounds sold. The area is now a housing estate.

**The line under construction, showing one of the troublesome tight curves that prevented ambulance trains reaching the hospital grounds.**

# QUEEN MARY'S HOSPITAL FOR CHILDREN

*Also known as:*
**Southern Hospital**
**Children's Infirmary**
**Orchard Hill Hospital**

The Queen Mary's Hospital for Children has the most unusual hospital railway featured in this book. Its sole purpose was to provide fun and pleasure.

The hospital was built in Carshalton in 1906 as a convalescent fever hospital. However, when ready for opening it was no longer needed for its original purpose. So it stood empty for three years. Then the Metropolitan Asylums Board suggested that they take over the hospital for the care of sick children in London. They realised the advantages of moving sick children to the fresh air of the country (as it was at that time) and opened the hospital in 1909. At this time over one in every hundred babies died in their first day of life and nearly four in every hundred died before they were one, of those that reached their first birthday one in every hundred died before their tenth birthday. In 1914 Queen Mary became the patron and the hospital was re-named Queen Mary's Hospital for Children.

The hospital became renowned for developments in the treatment of polio and cerebral palsy. In the Second World War the hospital gained a most unenviable record. It was the most heavily bombed hospital in the country. This led to the evacuation of the children to safer places. After the war the advances in medicine meant a decline in children's diseases such as TB and polio. This allowed children with learning disabilities from the Fountain Hospital in Tooting to be transferred to Queen Mary's in 1959.

In 1968 John Fowles, a local resident, approached the hospital with the offer to lay some ten and a quarter inch gauge track in the hospital grounds and run his miniature steam locomotives. The railway had been at Brockenhurst for twelve years under the name of "Meadow End Light Railway", collecting funds for the International League for Protection of Horses. The Hospital Management Committee agreed on condition that he gave free rides to the children staying at the hospital. This was readily

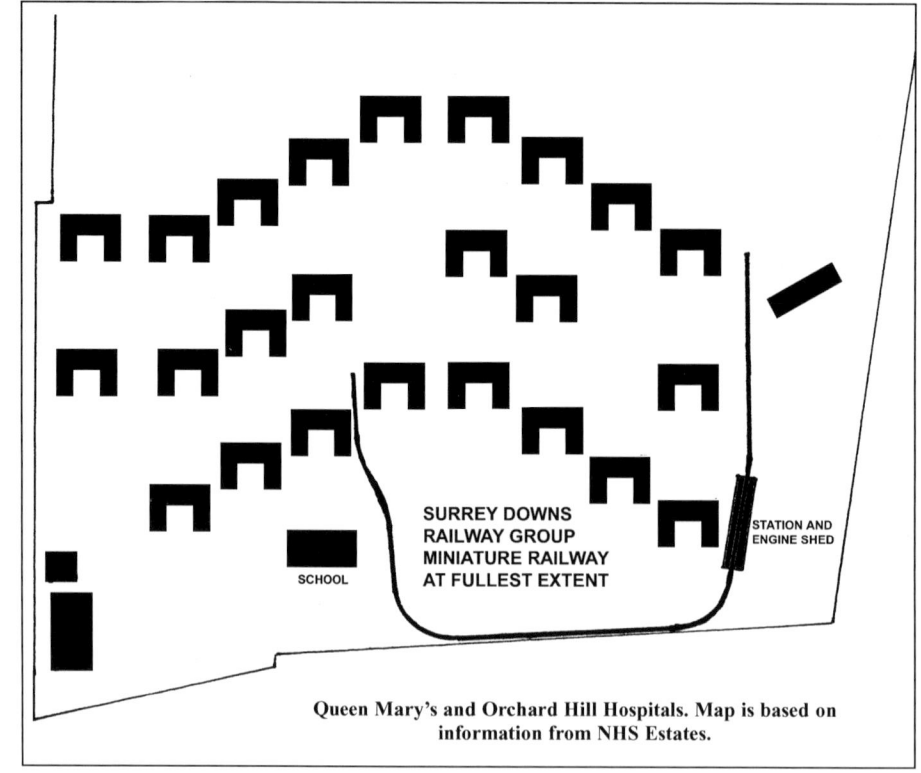

Queen Mary's and Orchard Hill Hospitals. Map is based on information from NHS Estates.

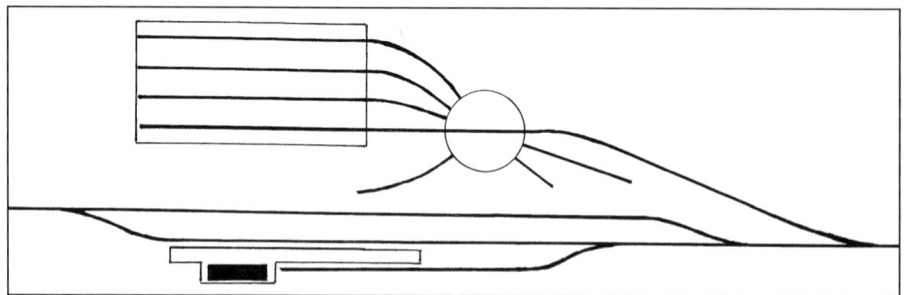

Miniature railway station and engine shed.

given and the half mile long line was laid in the grounds. The League of Friends of the hospital gave valuable assistance during this time.

The steam railway was a great success with the children and their parents as well as proving an attraction to the general public. It was open for running between May and September every Sunday afternoon. All were welcome, though on the understanding that priority was given to the hospital children.

In the early 1970s it was found that St Ebbas hospital in Epsom was too full to take the number of children with learning disabilities needing care. So a new hospital was opened on the St Mary's site, Orchard Hill Hospital, to care for adults with learn-

An early view of the railway with a steam locomotive hauling a train full of children who were patients from Queen Mary's Hospital.

The train has just run along the hospital boundary and is turning towards the station.

**A train full of happy children as it passes the school in the background.**

ing disabilities, allowing children to continue to be cared for as they grew older.

In 1971 John Fowles retired and moved away from the area, taking his steam locomotives with him. As the other enthusiasts who helped run the line were still willing to continue, the rest of the track, carriages and a diesel locomotive were purchased by the League of Friends. The group formed themselves into the Surrey Downs Railway Group and continued to run the railway and in 1974 extended the line and added a new terminus station by the hospital school. Two more locomotives joined the stud, a model of a British Rail "Hymek" Class 47 diesel, bought for the hospital by the local Scout Group in 1982. Built by Mardyke Miniature Railways Ltd at their factory in Rainham, Essex, it was given the name "Queen Scout". The other locomotive was Toby the Tram Engine, a battery powered engine made by Barry Jones, one of the group in 1983.

In 1993 St Mary's Hospital closed and patients were transferred to a new St Mary's hospital that was part of the St Helier's Hospital site, the main hospital in Carshalton. However Orchard Hill Hospital was kept and the railway now gave rides to the children and adults at the hospital.

So the railway ran happily into its 29th year at the hospital, giving enormous pleasure to everyone. In 1996 there was a major reorganisation in the NHS and the then Regional Health Authorities (RHAs) were removed. These had been responsible for hospital land and buildings on behalf of the Secretary of State. With the removal of the RHAs the responsibility for the NHS estate went to a new body called the NHS Estates Executive, a Civil Service body. When the Executive discovered that Queen Mary's Hospital had a miniature railway they stepped in quickly and ordered its removal. The last day of operation of the railway was 25 May 1997. The track was then lifted and removed.

The future for the hospital itself was also to go through a rocky period. The Merton, Sutton and Wandsworth Health Authority chose to re-organise the health services for those with learning difficulties and announced the closure of Orchard Hill. This was challenged by judicial review by some of the parents of the patients. The judge ruled that the Health Authority had acted unlawfully and the closure notice was repealed. The hospital is still open, though without its railway.

**The Hymek diesel donated by the local scout group when John Fowles moved away from the area.**

# ROYAL LANCASTER INFIRMARY

The Royal Lancaster Infirmary was founded in 1781. It occupied various premises up to the 1888s, when it occupied inadequate premises in Thurnham Street. The industrialist and Member of Parliament, Norval Helme gave Springfield Hall and grounds to the hospital. Public subscription was raised to build a new hospital on the site. The new hospital was opened in 1896 by the Duke and Duchess of York.

The railway came to Lancaster in 1840 when the Lancaster and Preston Junction Railway (L&PJR) reached the city from Preston. The line terminated at a station alongside the grounds of Springfield Hall. The terminus station had a four-track layout with platforms only on the outer tracks. There was also a coal yard and a goods warehouse. The Lancaster and Carlisle Railway (L&CR) was authorised in 1844 and opened in 1846. The route north started just before the terminus in Lancaster, sweeping west around the central built up area. A new station to serve the city was built and called Lancaster Castle Station. The then operators of the L&PJR, the Lancaster Canal Company, refused to pass the management of their railway to the L&CR. This meant there was joint management of the line to Preston. This unsatisfactory arrangement led to misunderstandings culminating in a crash between an L&CR express and an L&PJR slow train. The solution was to allow the L&CR to take over the management of both lines in 1849. This led to the terminus station being run down and it declined and was quickly closed to passengers, though it carried on with goods traffic until the late 1960s. By 1893 the terminus consisted of four sidings and a loop to a goods shed, all built on the old coal yard and to the west of

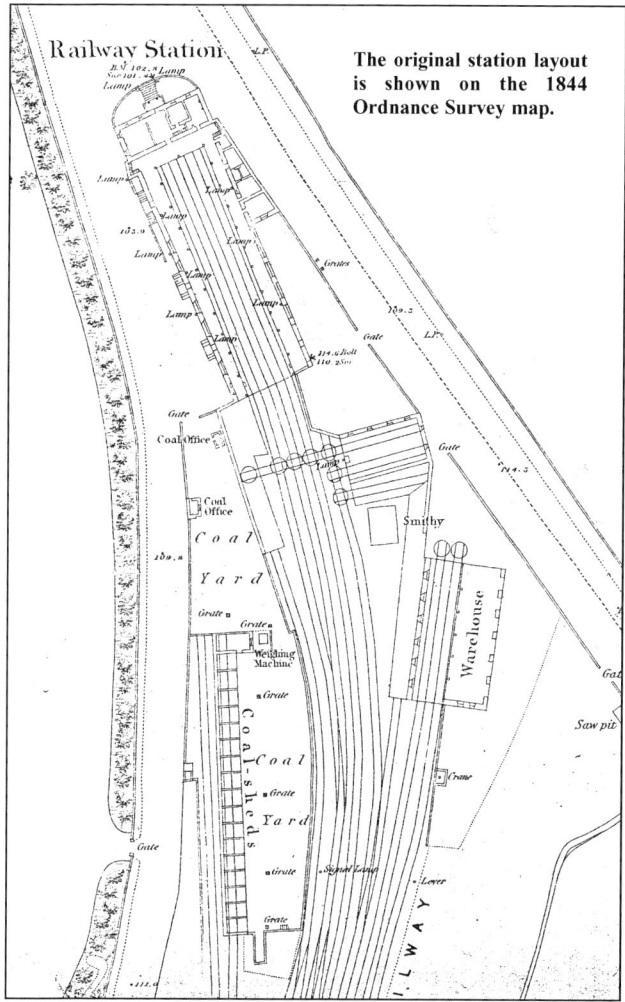

**The original station layout is shown on the 1844 Ordnance Survey map.**

**The original 1840 station building is now part of the Royal Lancaster Infirmary.**

the old passenger station. The land alongside South Road formerly used for the passenger service and the goods warehouse was sold for housing development. The old terminus building, but not the platforms, was kept. When the Royal Lancaster Infirmary was built a nurses' home was opened in the triangle of land between South Road and Ashton Road. The old terminus building was also used for nursing accommodation. As the need for nursing housing reduced the building became part of the office accommodation for the Infirmary.

This is the only known example of a hospital taking on redundant railway buildings.

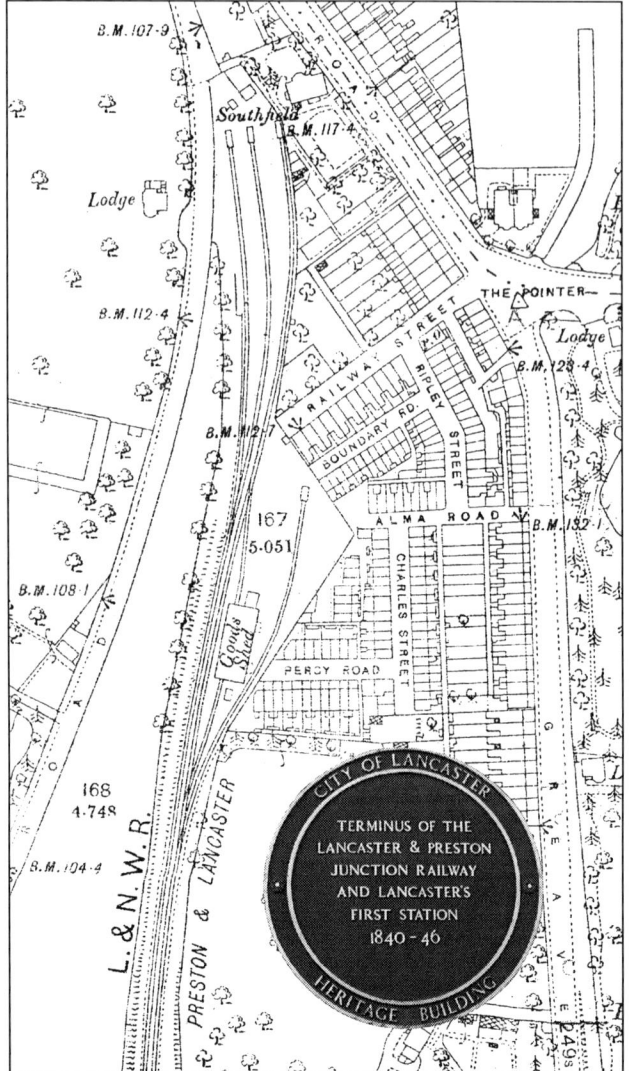

**The 1893 Ordnance Survey map shows the truncated station that was used after passenger services were withdrawn.**

# ST EDWARD'S HOSPITAL

*Also known as:*
**Cheddleton Hospital
Leek Brook Station
Staffordshire County Asylum
Staffordshire County Mental Hospital**

The Hospital was built as the Staffordshire County Asylum in the 1890s, opening in 1899. But before construction work began on the buildings the contractor prepared the track bed and laid rails in 1895 for his contractor's railway. This light railway used a small Manning Wardle Class H locomotive, named "Weaver", to take materials from the Churnet Valley line to the hospital site. Mention has been made in the introduction to the vast quantity of bricks and other materials needed to build this hospital. The contractors also had three or four small carriages and would take workers to and from Leek Station, so these were the first passengers to use the line.

When the hospital was completed in 1899 the contractor's

**The passenger tram with the locomotive with its first design of body. Later the body was reconstructed to resemble a greenhouse on wheels.**

**The locomotive before being rebuilt. It carries the monogram "SCC" for "Staffordshire Country Council".**

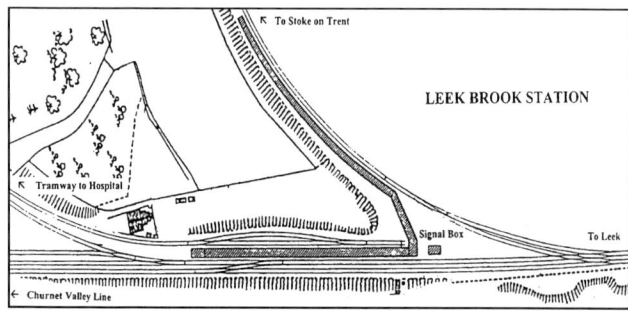

**Detail of the connection with the Churnet Valley Line.**

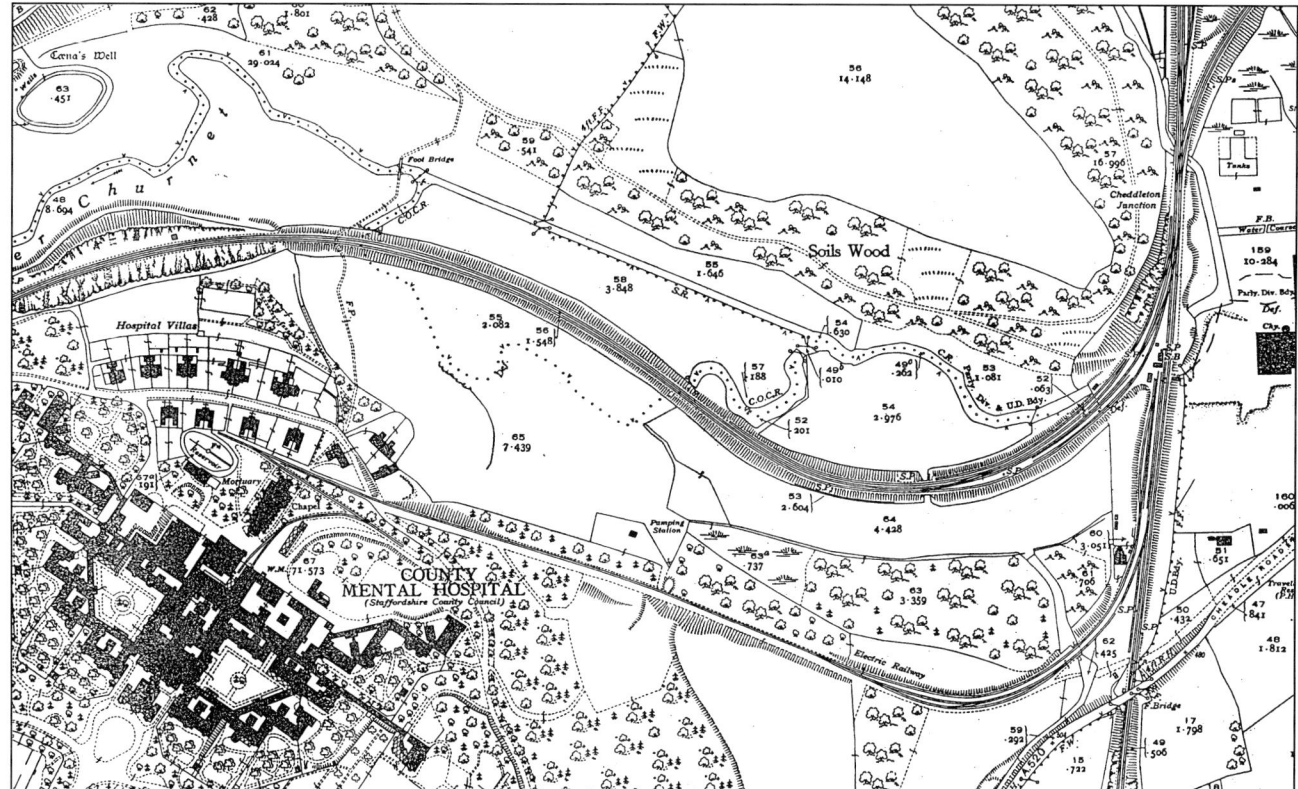
**St Edward's Hospital Tramway. Ordnance Survey 1925.**

railway was converted to an electric tramway. Electric overhead wire was erected and a platform was built on the Churnet Valley line of the North Staffordshire Railway. The platform was unusual as it was only accessible to up trains. This was given the name Leek Brook Station (or possibly Halt). An 0-4-0 electric locomotive was purchased from a factory in Wolverhampton. An old London County Council horse tram was purchased and converted to allow it to be hauled by the locomotive. This formed the passenger transport. Main line trains would stop at the platform and passengers for the hospital would alight and board the converted tramcar for the ride up the hill to the hospital. The purpose was primarily to take staff to work, but visitors to the hospital were allowed to use it and no charge was made. The line was entirely private and in the early days the locomotive and the tramcar had the letters SCC as a monogram indicating they were the property of Staffordshire County Council. The power for the line came from the hospital boiler house. There are stories that when demand for power was high in the hospital the tram would have to operate on reduced power and could only crawl along.

The line ran up the hill towards the hospital, to a stub end, where the train reversed to take a branch up to the hospital. The main use of the tramway was to take coal to the boiler house. Around 200 tons of coal were needed each month. The coal would be brought by the North Staffordshire Railway and left in the transfer siding, beside the platform. Main line locomotives were not allowed into the hospital grounds, because the track was lightly built and it was likely that a heavy locomotive would spread the rails and come off the track. Indeed in 1931 an LMS locomotive did stray on to the hospital side and found itself in trouble. In addition to the coal trucks, the line was also used to take wagons with produce to the kitchens.

Passenger operation finished in the 1920s and the old horse tramcar body was put on the cricket field to become the first pavilion. At the same time the body of the locomotive was given a cosmetic rebuild. The very open sides were enclosed, with lots of small windows, giving the whole thing the appearance of a greenhouse on wheels. As it now looked quite different some historians mistakenly thought that a new locomotive had been purchased. The rebuilt locomotive continued to haul coal up to the 1950s.

**The locomotive pushes two full coal wagons up the incline to the hospital boiler house.**

The last coal train is believed to have run on 16 December 1954 and the line then closed. The locomotive remained on the hospital grounds until it was sold as scrap in 1957 to Thomas Foden of Longton, who broke it up on site. The remains of Leek Brook platform can be seen and much of the track bed in the hospital grounds is very clear. The old tramway shed still exists and the original rails can be seen in the concrete floor. The hospital is intact and still in use.

**The coal was unloaded outside the hospital chapel, close to the boiler house. The wagon with the letters "SC" is not from Staffordshire County as first thought, but belongs to Stephenson Clarke a coal merchant based in London.**

# SCALEBOR PARK HOSPITAL

*Also known as:*
   **West Riding of Yorkshire County Asylum for Private Patients**
   **Scalebor Park Mental Hospital**
   **Scalebor Park**
   **Moor Lane Centre**

The West Riding of Yorkshire Lunacy Board decided in 1895 to purchase Scalebor Hall, near Burley in Wharfdale, with its estate of 120 acres, in order to build an asylum for private patients, just three miles from High Royds Hospital. The architect J. Vickers-Edwards was commissioned to design the hospital buildings and some £126,000 was set aside for its construction. The building work was contracted to Isaac Gold Ltd of Hunslet Leeds, who commenced building in 1897. In the course of the construction of the hospital two site railway systems were used. There was a standard gauge light railway that may have had a siding connection with the Midland Railway line just north of Burley in Wharfedale Station (that was adjacent to the hospital site). There was also a three-foot gauge line used on the site itself, which probably was not built until the following year. The first Ordnance Survey map after the commencement of building is the 1909 edition, seven years after the opening of the hospital. However, this does show a short railway line in the grounds of West Lodge, the other side of Moor Lane from the main hospital building. This may be the remnants of the railways used by the contractor on the site.

Isaac Gold Ltd used two locomotives on the standard gauge line. The first was an unnamed 0-4-0 saddle tank built in 1887 and the other a much more recently purchased 0-4-0 saddle tank named "Airdrie" that was built in 1894. The narrow gauge line used an 1898 0-4-0 saddle tank named "Hannah". The hospital was completed and opened in 1902. The two lines were lifted when the builder completed the contract, so they were another example of contractor's railways being used for the construction of the hospital, but then removed and not used by the hospital authorities.

Originally it was able to house 210 paying patients (105 of each sex in eight wards). Later it extended slightly to be able to treat 300 patients. What now seems bizarre to us, the medical practitioners at the time the hospital opened had the idea of curing general paralysis of the insane by injecting patients with malaria and a special small unit was built to undertake these experiments. Facilities included a modern administration block, a gymnasium, ballroom and in the beautiful grounds a football and cricket pitch, bowling greens and tennis courts.

It is unsure when the private payment for treatment ceased, but it is certain that after the hospital became part of the National Health Service in 1948 it was no longer a private hospital. In the 1960s a further four wards were added in a new building, bringing the total to twelve, with two bungalows added in the 1980s for the elderly mentally ill.

The hospital closed in 1995 as part of the Government initiative for the care of mentally ill people, much to the anger of staff

**Scalebor Park Hospital buildings when they were in use for the treatment of patients.**

and many in the community. Most of the buildings were demolished and the land was sold for housing development. Now called Scalebor Park the development included three blocks of converted hospital buildings; and terraced and detached housing, providing 139 new houses and flats.

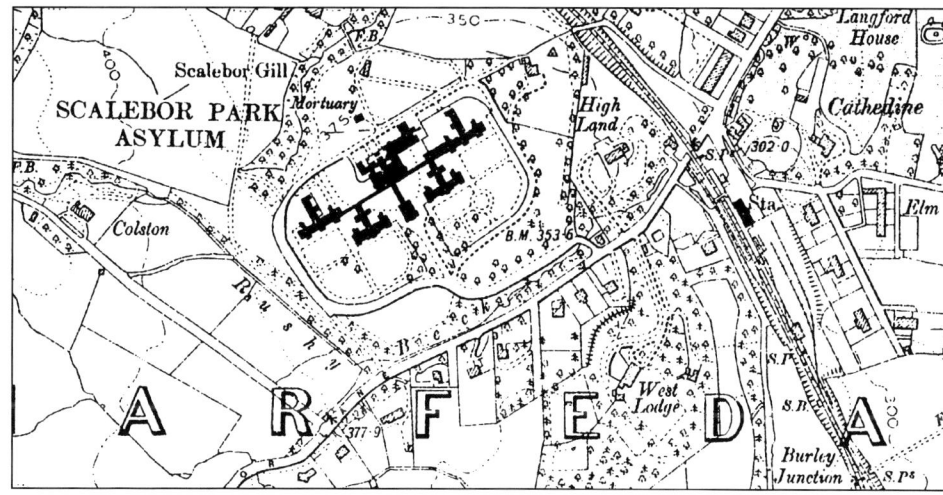

**Scalebor Park Hospital, Ordnance Survey 1909.**

# THREE COUNTIES HOSPITAL

*Also known as:*
**Three Counties Asylum**
**Fairfield Hospital**

In 1837 Hertfordshire and Huntingdonshire started sending their mentally ill poor to the Bedford Asylum, built in 1812. Within a few years it became clear that the facilities could not cope with the demands. In 1852 a survey was undertaken which recommended extending the asylum. This was too expensive so it was proposed that land be purchased as near to the Great Northern Railway (GNR) as possible to build a hospital for use by Bedfordshire, Cambridgeshire, Hertfordshire and Huntingdonshire. In the event Cambridge dropped out and so three counties took the proposal forward. In 1856 200 acres of land were purchased near Stotfold, some three miles north of Hitchin, with a further 57 acres for a connection to the road and the GNR. The railway connection was necessary to take building materials to the site. The laying of the track was contracted out to the GNR, but they did not want the new railway to connect

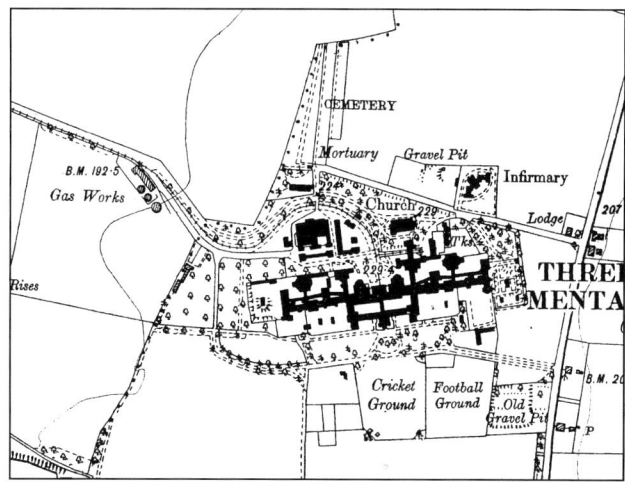

**Detail of the railway and hospital buildings. Note the Gas Works that was the main reason for the railway. Ordnance Survey 1926.**

**The only photograph we have of the railway in the grounds is this uninspiring view of the main gate with the light railway alongside the road.**

with their main line. So the hospital authorities purchased the existing siding and weighing machine from the Arlesey Cement Company. It had been calculated that the use of the railway would be £1,000 cheaper than using road access, just during the building of the hospital. The line ran from the siding to the hospital with a short siding at the gas house.

The railway had been completed by June 1857 by contractor William Webster and so construction of the hospital buildings could begin. Some 30,000 tons of material were carried to the site. The hospital opened in 1860. The railway was then taken over by the hospital authorities and it carried goods, mainly coal, from the main line to the hospital. In the early days the hospital had its own passenger carriage, but this was replaced by a horse drawn omnibus around 1863. There is no record of it ever having carried any passengers after this date. The GNR built a large railway station at the junction and this was opened in 1886 and called Arlesey Siding. The station had four platforms and the complex included sidings to a brick works. The station was renamed Three Counties in 1886. Patients, staff and visitors travelling by rail would arrive at the main line station. From here they would walk or travel by road to the hospital.

In 1876 there was a major railway accident at Arlesey Sidings. On 23 December a locomotive had been shunting wagons, a manoeuvre that involved crossing the main line to fetch wagons and back across to join the main train. On returning back across the main line three wagons derailed blocking the whole line. An express train was heading south and was travelling too fast to stop at the home signal. Five persons died in the resulting crash including the driver of the express. The cause of the accident was a signalman's error and this with other similar accidents led to the adoption of the block system of train control.

Hospital goods traffic would arrive by rail at the main line station and then be shunted into the exchange siding. The line was on an upward slope to the hospital, so wagons would be shunted by the GNR just on to hospital property where hospital staff would use a horse to haul them to the gas works. The empty wagons would then be gravity shunted back to the main line for collection. A new gas holder was built in 1911 and the tramway was relaid.

During the First World War the hospital took patients from Norfolk Asylum, which had been converted to a military hospital. Later in the war soldiers suffering from shell-shock were taken by Three Counties for treatment. Expansion of the hospital continued and by 1936 the grounds covered 410 acres. Revenue from the farm helped to subsidise the costs of the hospital. In the Second World War the patients were transferred to other hospitals and the Three Counties became a general hospital taking people from London, as the hospitals in London were considered to be at a high risk of bomb damage. At the end

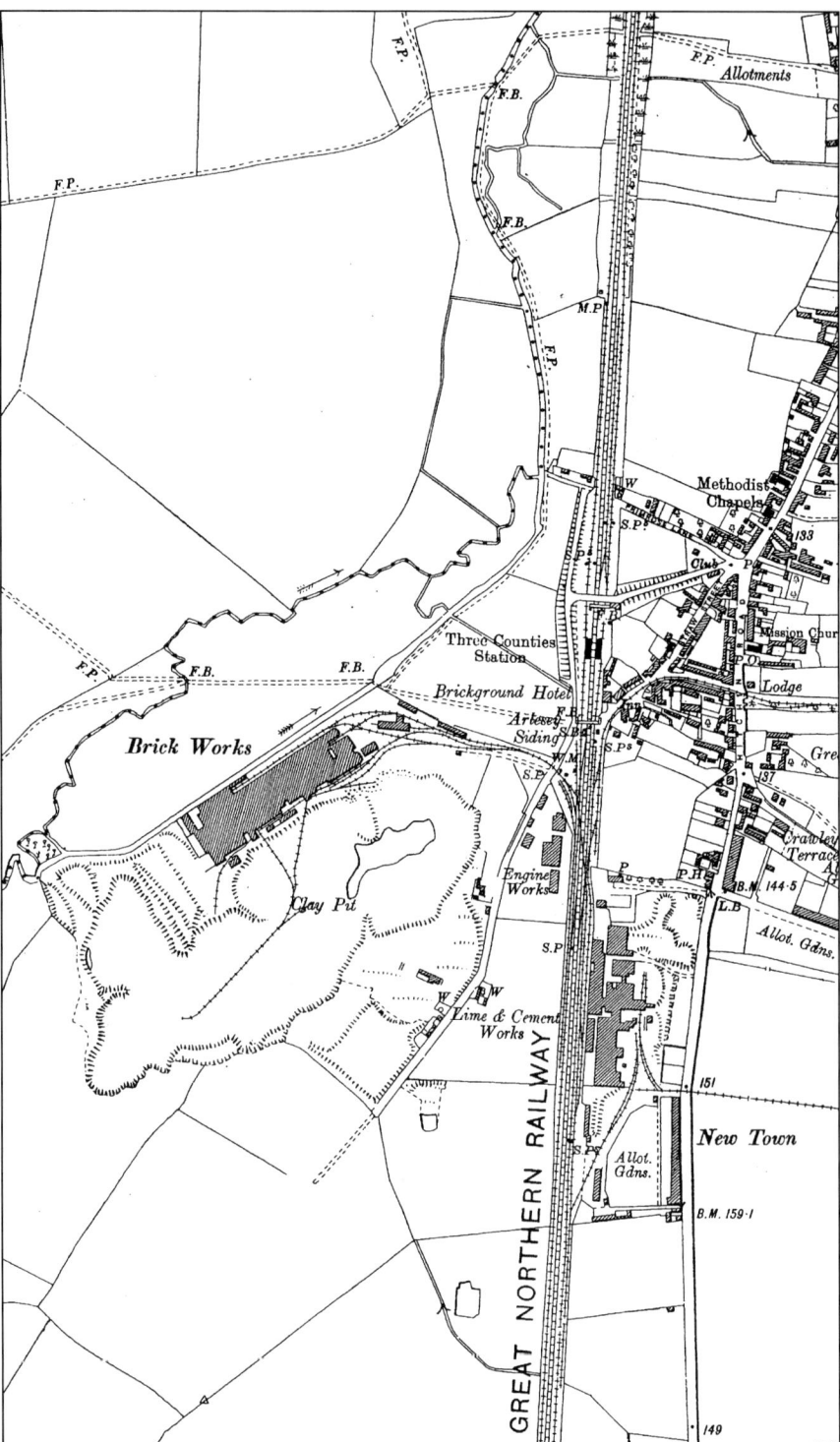

**The Three Counties Hospital Railway. Ordnance Survey 1926.**

of the war the hospital returned to its normal function, just ready to be absorbed into the National Health Service in 1948.

In 1952 the hospital gas works was demolished, having been allowed to deteriorate until it was in a dangerous state. This was the end for the hospital railway, as its prime purpose of bringing coal to the gas works had now disappeared. So it was closed and the line sold for scrap. Three Counties Station continued for a few more years, finally closing in 1959.

The hospital itself continued to serve the community until 1999 when it was closed under the government's Care in the Community initiative. The site was subsequently sold and is now being developed as a housing estate.

**Three Counties Station, the line to the hospital goes left between the station and the tall chimneys of the cement works, but is hidden by buildings.**

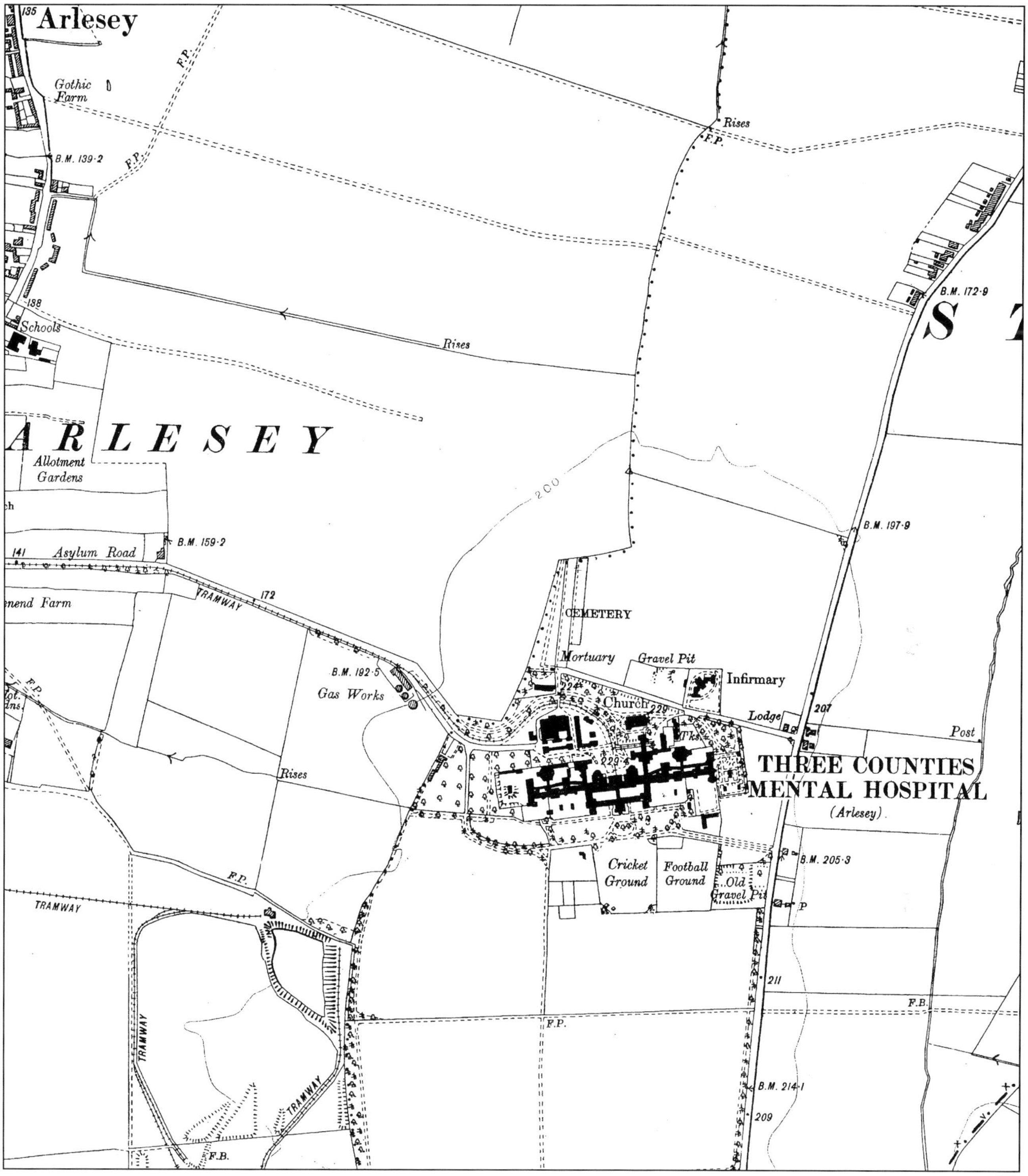
Arlesey
Gothic Farm
Schools
ARLESEY
Allotment Gardens
Asylum Road
TRAMWAY
Gas Works
Rises
CEMETERY
Mortuary
Gravel Pit
Infirmary
Church
Lodge
Post
THREE COUNTIES MENTAL HOSPITAL
(Arlesey)
Cricket Ground
Football Ground
Old Gravel Pit
F.P.
F.B.

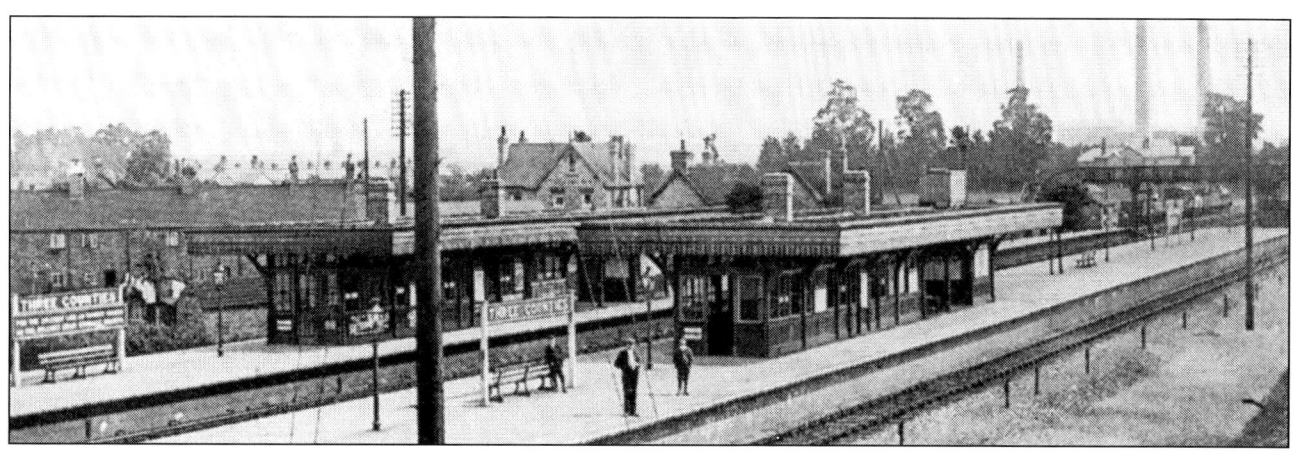

# WHITTINGHAM HOSPITAL

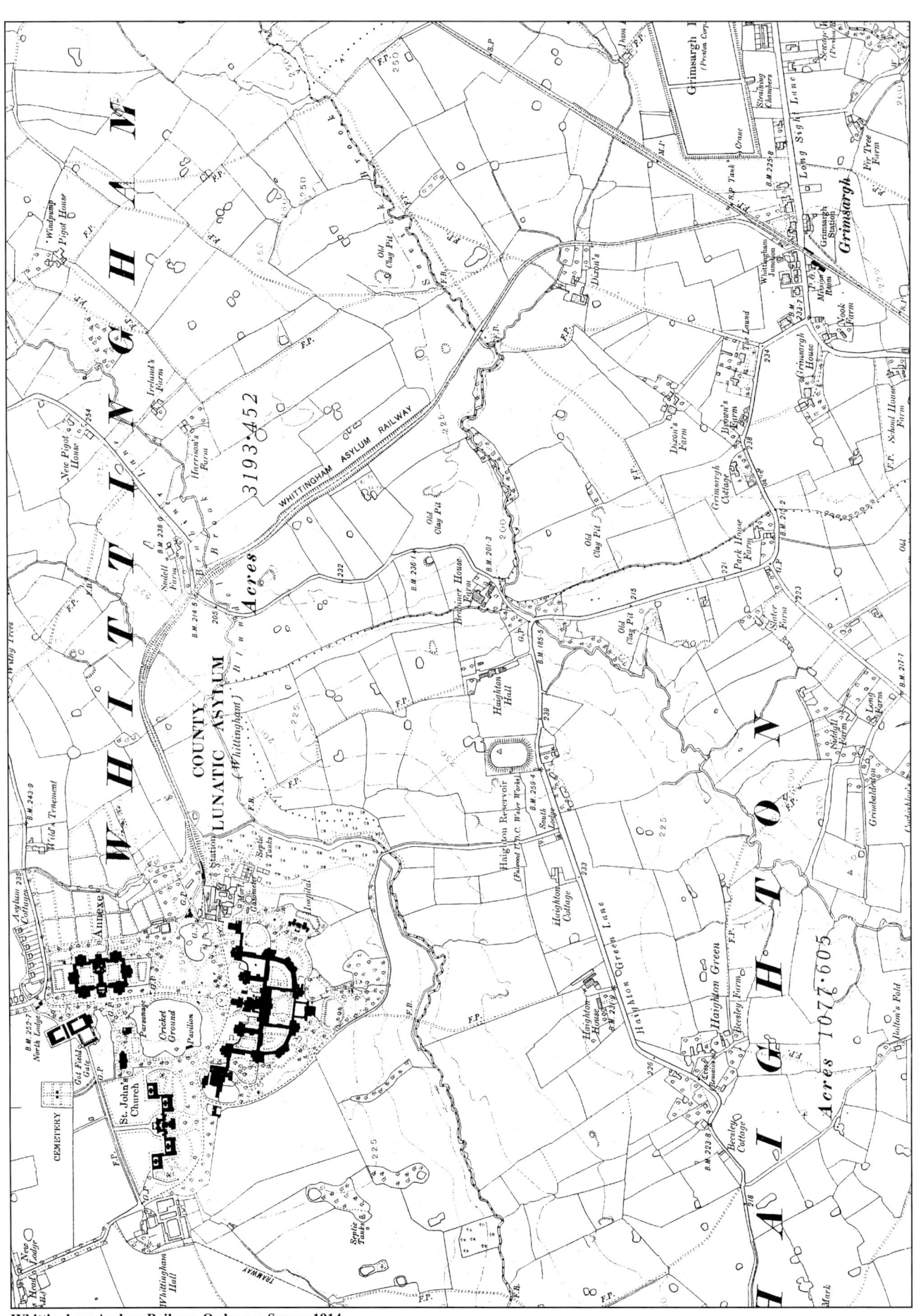

**Whittingham Asylum Railway. Ordnance Survey 1914.**

*Also known as:*
> **County Mental Hospital**
> **Grimsargh**
> **Lancashire County Mental Asylum**

The county of Lancashire realised in 1866 that the provision of accommodation for pauper lunatics was far short of the demand. Proposals were made for the building of a new asylum. Land was chosen that was near the village of Grimsargh, some five miles north east of Preston. The site was one and a half miles from the village and the Preston and Longridge Railway (opened in 1840). So in 1869 157 acres of land were purchased and building of the 1,000-bedded hospital began. Clay was dug from the site and the bricks for the buildings were made by the labourers constructing the hospital. Although there was a railway line less than two miles away, all the materials for the building were brought by road from Preston or Longridge. The construction took four years and the first patients were admitted in 1873. All hospital supplies, including the tons of coal for the boiler house, were brought by horse and cart. This was very expensive as many men had to be employed just to bring the supplies to the hospital, as well as many horses and vehicles.

But it was not until 1884 that suggestions were made to link the hospital with the station at Grimsargh. After protracted negotiations with the railway company, and with local farmers for the purchase of the necessary land for the line, the nearly two miles long line was opened in 1889. The cost of building the line included the purchase of a locomotive and two wagons. The locomotive was a Barclay 0-4-0 saddle tank. Initially the line was goods only, but soon the idea of carrying passengers was suggested. A carriage was purchased from the Lancaster Wagon Company and the passenger service began. From the beginning the railway was to be a proper private railway, run entirely by the hospital management and called the Whittingham Hospital Railway (WHR). Initially the single line railway entered the hospital grounds and ended at a buffer stop. By 1914 a station had been built at the boundary of the hospital. It was covered over, including the track, and had a platform for passengers. An open platform was built at Grimsargh Station on the private railway line for passengers, with a small waiting room. At the hospital the line had been continued beyond the station to some goods sidings by hospital buildings. Unusually for a railway, passengers were carried free. This included members of the public. Access to the stations was made available to anyone, whether they had business with the hospital or not.

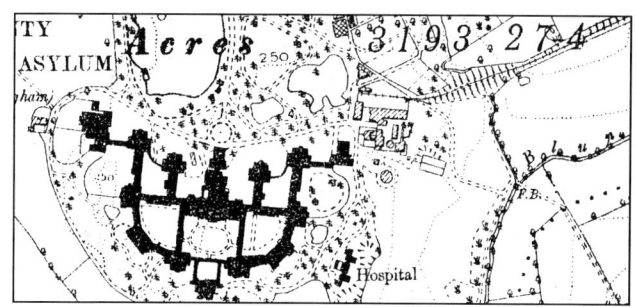

**The development of the railway at the hospital. This Ordnance Survey map for 1895 shows a plain stub end just inside the hospital grounds.**

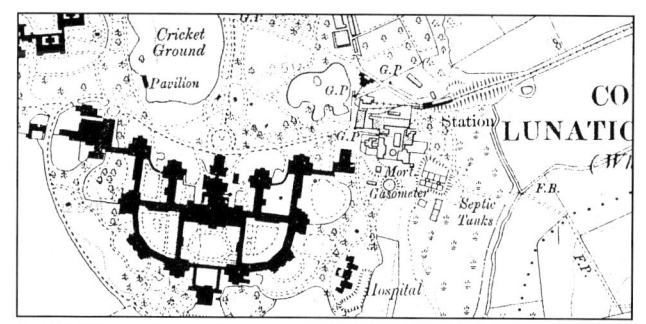

**By 1914 the Ordnance Survey map shows that the station has been built and a siding constructed.**

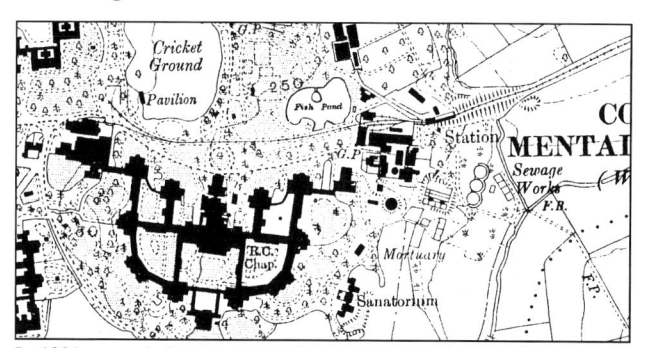

**In 1921 a new boiler house was built the other side of the hospital and the line extended across the grounds to reach it. Ordnance Survey 1932.**

The locomotive and rolling stock carried the letters CAW, standing for County Asylum Whittingham. Five extra carriages were purchased, second-hand from other railways. In 1904 the Barclay locomotive was joined by another, this time an 0-4-2.

**The locomotive retrieves the passenger vans from the siding to take them to the hospital station for the next run to Grimsargh.**

They were given the numbers 1 and 2 respectively.

In 1921 a new extension was built from the goods sidings in the hospital to the new boiler house. It crossed the hospital gardens and lawns, to the boiler house and was used for goods traffic only. Strangely the main line railway closed for passenger use in 1930, but the hospital carried on taking passengers for a further 27 years until the line closed in 1957. The original carriages ran until the end of the Second World War. They were replaced with three ex-LNWR goods brake vans. Hospital carpenters converted the vans for passenger use. The ends were enclosed and windows cut in the side.

In 1947 locomotive number 1 came to the end of its life. The hospital searched for a suitable replacement and purchased Southern Railway number 2357 (named Riddlesdown) an 0-4-2 tank engine from the D1 class. One of Stroudley's engines, the locomotive was actually older than the Whittingham Railway. On entering service at Whittingham, the locomotive was renamed James Fryar after the Chairman of the Hospital Committee and given the number CMHW No 3, the letters standing for County Mental Hospital Whittingham. The engine had difficulty on the sharp bends of the line. The second Barclay engine needed replacing in 1952 and a second-hand Sentinel locomotive was purchased from Bolton Gas Works.

The locomotive James Fryar became unserviceable in 1956. At this time the line had been running down, as most deliveries to the hospital were now being made by road. As they decided to close the line a petrol crisis meant that it carried on for a further six months. But the end came in 1957. At its busiest the railway carried 3,000 passengers a week, with twelve trains each day, though there was no Sunday service. The goods traffic amounted to over 12,000 tons per year. At its largest Whittingham had over 3,000 patients and was the largest mental hospital in Europe.

The hospital closed in the mid 1990s and the patients moved to other accommodation. The future of the hospital site is still under debate. Two proposals for housing development have been rejected, but the local council has included the development of the site for housing in its future plans.

**The sidings just beyond the hospital station. The central track leads to the extension and the new boiler house.**

**The extension to the new boiler house had to run through the hospital gardens. The horticulture seems better than the track laying.**

**Whittingham Hospital Station with its overall roof. Access to the boiler house was through the station.**

**The hospital passenger train leaves Grimsargh Station, branching off to the hospital. The carriages are the ex-LNWR guards vans converted by the hospital carpenters for passenger use.**

# WARTIME TEMPORARY MILITARY HOSPITALS IN ENGLAND

**World War 1 ambulance train.**

During the First and Second World Wars the demand for hospital care for wounded troops vastly outstripped the capacity available. So in addition to the War Office commandeering many psychiatric hospitals, a large number of temporary hospitals, or hospital camps, were built. In the First World War a total of 171 hospitals have been identified that were used for the care of military wounded. It is probable that a similar number were requisitioned or built during the Second World War.

During the First World War military trains were grouped into four categories. "Imperial A" was the top category and such trains were to be run at high speed with a completely clear passage. Nothing was allowed to impede their path. "Imperial B" trains had precedence over all civilian and other military

**A newly built ambulance carriage with its attendants c.1917.**

**US troops in front of a new ambulance carriage, Doncaster Carriage and Wagon Works.**

trains. "Imperial C" trains had precedence over civilian trains, but not other military trains and "Imperial D" did not have precedence over civilian trains, but were required to be given the best possible journey. The "Imperial A and B" category was usually reserved for trains carrying the King, Heads of State and the very top military officers.

There were a number of ambulance trains available at the beginning of the First World War. But it was soon evident that there was a far greater demand than existing trains could cope with. As a stopgap existing passenger carriages, often old stock, were pressed into use. Brackets were fitted to take two tiers of beds and drinking water tanks were installed. This was done in haste and often could be completed in a couple of days. More purpose-built ambulance carriages were ordered from carriage works around Britain. Throughout the Wartime period the South-Eastern and Chatham Railway ran 7,515 ambulance trains from Dover Marine Station alone.

During the Second World War the railways in Britain were very much unrecognised heroes. Many of the railway staff had been conscripted into the army to fight the war. This left a depleted number of drivers, firemen and other staff to run a railway system that was stretched to its very limit. The staff had to cope with bomb damaged lines, trains and stations, while keeping the lines running to take workers to and from their factories, all contributing to the war effort. In addition they had to cope with strict blackout conditions, making driving a train at night a frightening experience. The cab was wrapped in tarpaulin to prevent the fire being seen by enemy bombers. The towns and countryside were pitch black. So the trains would hurtle along the track with the driver and fireman unable to see anything. If they were caught in a bombing raid they were advised to stop the train and seek what shelter they could, but most just carried on driving. On top of the normal traffic they also had to deal with massive troop movements and

**Interior of a 1914 ambulance train.**

**Ambulance train in Liverpool Lime Street Station about 1917.**

getting vital munitions from factories all over Britain to the docks.

Two major examples of the situations that the railways had to handle were Dunkirk and D-day. During the Dunkirk evacuation thousands and thousands of troops crossed the channel to ports all along the south coast. During these days the Southern Railway was virtually closed to all civilian passenger trains. The railways ran special troop trains to disperse them in an orderly fashion to camps in England, Wales and Scotland. The other example was in the reverse direction. D-Day meant gathering troops from everywhere and taking them to the south coast, with all the tons of equipment and munitions they needed. Railway workers often worked around the clock with just the odd snatched sleep.

One of the important tasks was to run ambulance trains taking injured troops from ships to a variety of hospital facilities around the country. In the history of many of the mental institutions in this book there is a note of the hospital being used for military casualties during the World Wars. In addition many temporary units were built to house more injured. The ambulance trains were given priority to ensure as swift a journey as possible to the hospital.

The hospitals given in this section are examples of the types of hospitals that gave invaluable service during wartime. All those with railway lines that entered the hospital camp grounds are included. However, I have not been able to identify all those

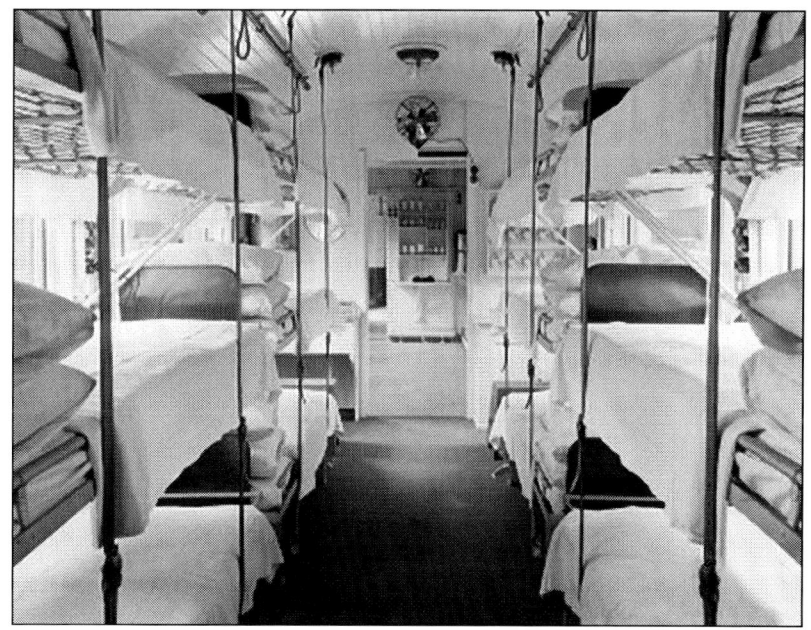

**Interior of ambulance train 1917.**

hospital camps that were located close to a rail link, but that had no line within the camp. So I have included a few as examples of the many. The stories they have can be repeated for many such hospital camps.

For a more detailed account of the role of railways in wartime Britain I recommend "War on the Line" by Bernard Darwin, published by The Southern Railway Company in 1946, and reprinted by Middleton Press in 1984 and 1993.

# BEWDLEY USA MILITARY HOSPITAL

The USA military camps and hospitals at Bewdley, Worcestershire, are used as an example of the crucial links between the railways and hospitals during wartime.

In 1942 land owned by Kidderminster Borough was requisitioned by the War Office for two army camps. The land was close to the railway station at Stourport and indeed the line ran alongside one of the camps. The camps were ready to take their first troops by November 1943. The camps were used by USA troops and by the summer of 1944 there were 4,000 in the two camps. A further 10,000 were spread around tented camps within a few miles. These formed part of over 1.5 million American troops in this country.

After D-Day the camps became military hospitals, designated as the 297th General Hospital with nearly 1,500 beds and the 114th General Hospital with a similar number of beds.

Wounded soldiers would arrive in Britain by ship and transfer to ambulance trains. These would travel to one of the many hospital camps that there were around Britain. As the train approached the designated station, about half an hour ride away, a medical officer and a surgical officer would board it. They would go through the train fixing labels on each patient identifying which ward they were to go to at the hospital.

On arrival at the station eight men would be allocated to each carriage. Four would go aboard and transfer patients to stretchers and carry them to the doors. The stretcher would be handed to the other four on the ground, who would load the patient onto an ambulance for travel to the hospital. Walking wounded would be helped off the carriages and to the ambulances.

**Bewdley Camp with a train passing by on the railway line in the background.**

41

The Bewdley Hospitals were open for about a year and between them treated around 15,000 patients. Today there is little to see of these camps. A housing estate has been built on the site of the 297th General Hospital, while the 114th General Hospital is part of a nature reserve and some foundations are just visible through the undergrowth. These are typical of many hundreds of similar hospitals throughout the British Isles. Most were located within easy reach of a railway station to enable the quick transfer of patients.

The aerial photograph of the camp seems to indicate that wooden platforms were erected alongside the railway south of the level crossing. It is possible that trains would go directly to the camp and the wounded soldiers transferred with minimum disruption to the wards.

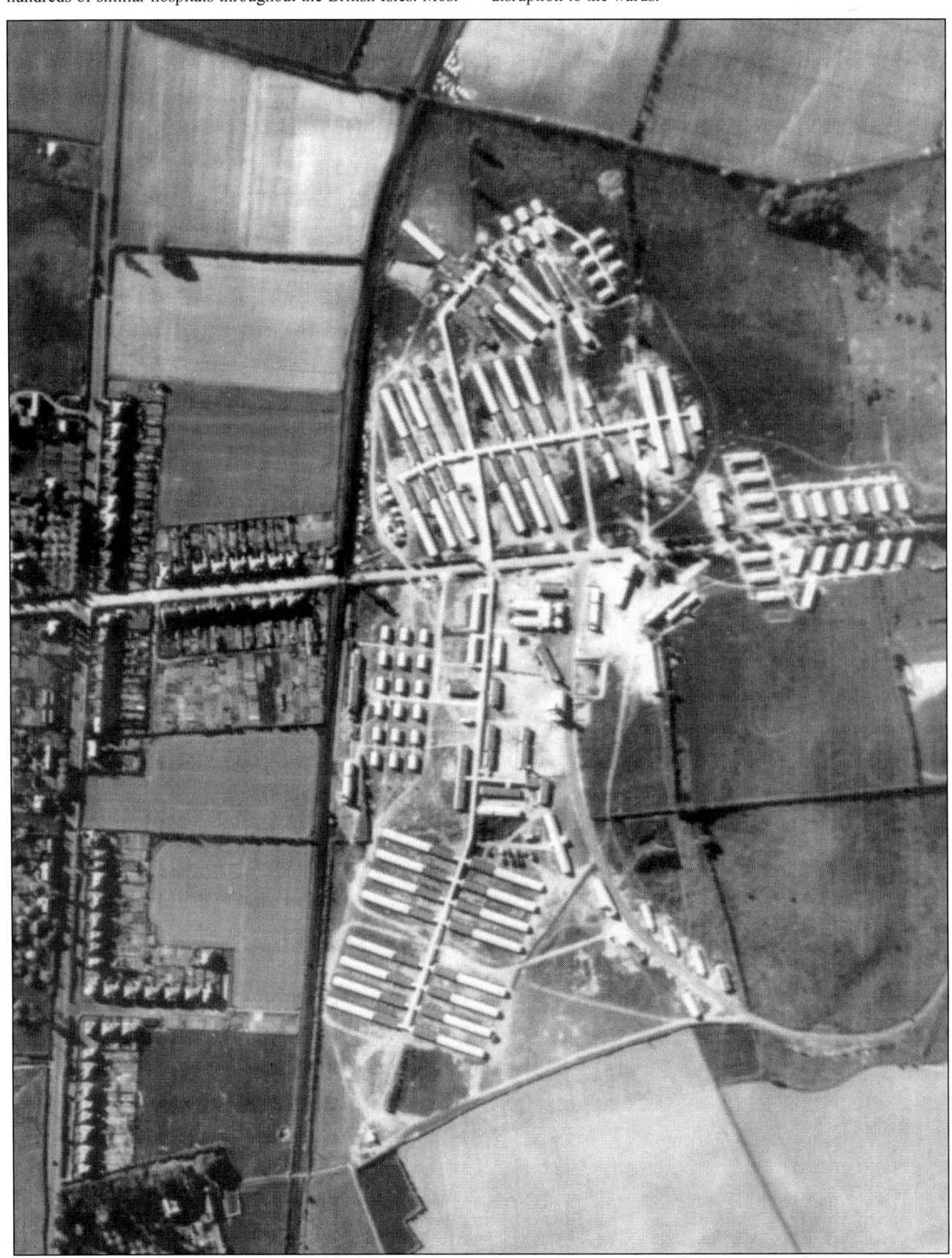

**This aerial view of Bewdley Camp shows the extent of the site. Just below the level crossing there appear to be wooden platforms alongside the railway line.**

# BULFORD CAMP MILITARY HOSPITAL

In 1898 the War Office purchased 1,917 acres of the Bulford Manor Estate. At the same time 751 acres were purchased from another nearby estate. A further 2,205 acres in and around Brigmerston were added in 1899, while in 1900 another 288 acres were purchased in Bulford. From the very beginning tented camps were set up, forming the start of Bulford Camp. The impact of such a large number of young men in a small village must have been considerable. In 1901 there were over 1,000 troops and just over 300 villagers. From 1900 the camp was improved with the building of wooden huts including the provision of a 50-bedded hospital.

**Amesbury Station showing the branch right that leads to Bulford Camp.**

The London and South Western Railway (LSWR) planned to build a branch line from Grately on the Basingstoke to Salisbury line to Lavington via Amesbury, Shrewton and Tileshead. The line to Amesbury was opened to passengers in 1902. This short line was the very first railway in Britain to have automatic signalling. The War Office then objected to the remainder of the line being built as they wanted the land to be available for army training. As the work had already started at Amesbury Station for the extension the land was used to provide more sidings. The Station itself was very large with extensive sidings and a turntable. There was a Station Master's house and cottages for the railway workers. With the development of Bulford Camp the LSWR proposed to continued building work to extend the line from Amesbury to Bulford. This was approved and the extension opened in 1906. Bulford Station had goods sidings and a cattle pen, as well as the usual station buildings. The railway was then extended into the camp with a large platform being built close to the hospital. Three locomotives were used on the line, all 0-6-0 saddle tanks and named "Salisbury", "Westminster" and "Bembridge" (an ex-Isle of Wight Railway engine). "Westminster" was sent to the Fovant Military Railway in 1917, leaving just the other two locomotives to run the line.

Following the outbreak of war in 1914 the camp was extended to the north by the British Section of the New Zealand Expeditionary Force. They soon left and the work was continued by Canadian forces. New Zealand troops occupied the camp extension in 1916 and it became known as ANZAC Camp. A

**Amesbury Station looking towards Grately.**

**The platform at Bulford Camp with a railway special tour.**

43

new hospital was built next to the existing one, but significantly larger, having 950 beds.

At the end of the First World War it took many months to repatriate the New Zealand troops. Many were housed at Bulford Camp, still under wartime discipline and training. This created enormous resentment and there was fear of rebellion. One of the officers suggested that rather than square bashing the troops could cut a Kiwi, the emblem of New Zealand, on the side of Beacon Hill. The hill had a chalk underlay below an earth cover. The kiwi was drawn out with the letters "NZ" alongside. The whole picture covers an area of one and a half acres and is 420 feet high. After the War the upkeep of the emblem was financed by Kiwi Products (UK) Ltd, best known for shoe polish. But they were unable to continue after 1967, so the New Zealand High Commission took over for ten years. After this time financial support ceased

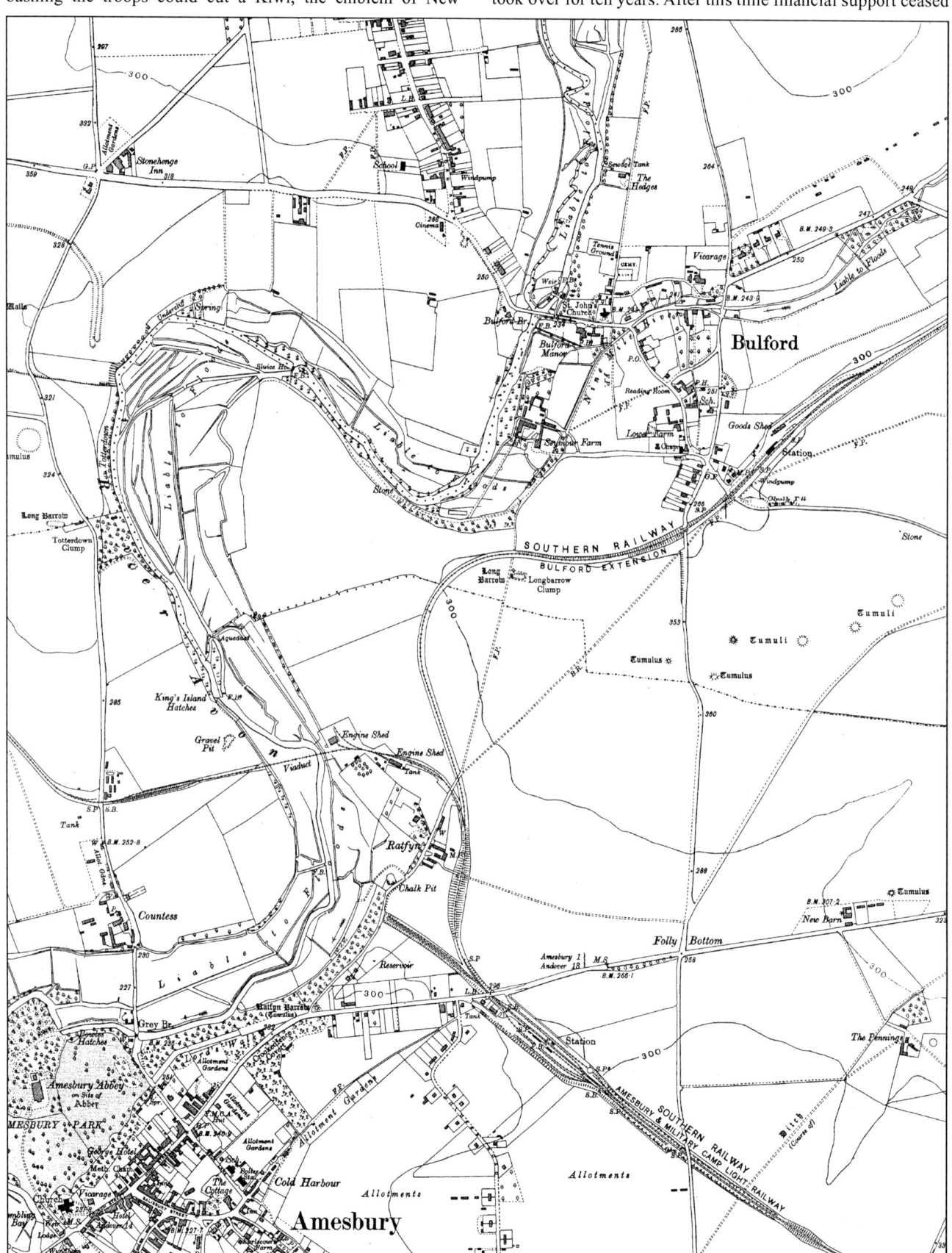

**Bulford Camp Railway, from Amesbury Camp to Bulford. The branch on the left leads to Larkhill Military Railway. Ordnance Survey 1925.**

and the emblem started to deteriorate. In 1980 249 Signal Squadron of the Royal Signals undertook the restoration of the site and they continue to maintain the Kiwi twice every year.

At the end of the First World War the temporary camp was gradually dismantled, though it was not until the mid to late 1920s that the final huts were cleared. This left the main permanent camp. The hospital was still in use in 1921, but by 1929 it was used only as a reception station and it had disappeared by 1939. The railway continued to play a role in the Second World War, moving troops and supplies, but without the hospital it was not used to move wounded troops.

Public services on the railway finished in 1952. Goods traffic ended in 1963 and the track lifted in 1965. In 1969 the Property Services Agency built offices on the Bulford Station site and they erected a signal on the approach road as a reminder that the site used to be the station.

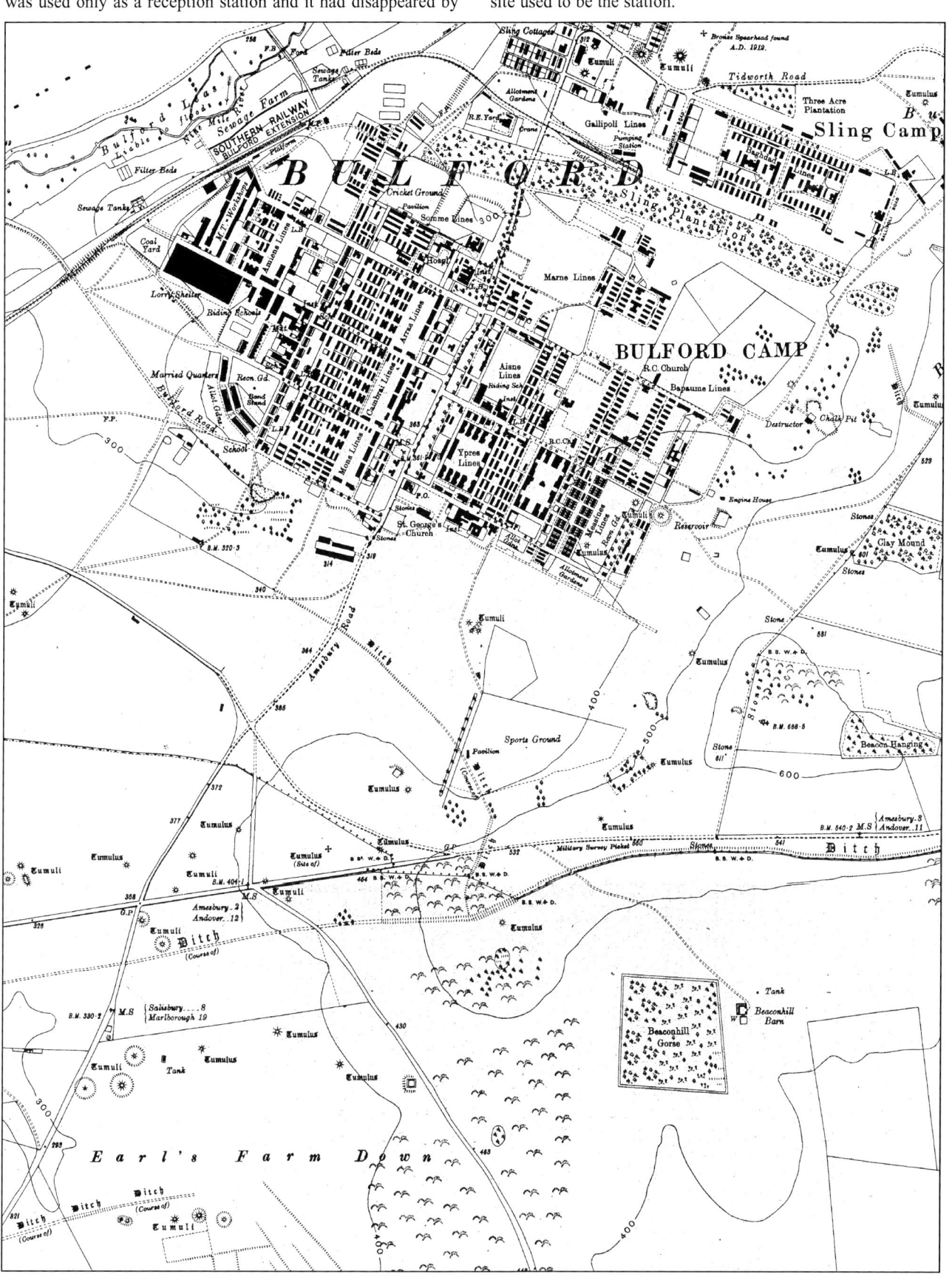

Codford Railway with the location of the hospital camp. Railway superimposed on Ordnance Survey map of 1926.

46

# CODFORD CAMP MILITARY HOSPITAL

**The station in Codford Camp, showing the simple nature of the line.**

In September 1914 the quiet villages of Codford St Peter and Codford St Mary with a population of around 500 suddenly found themselves invaded by troops readying themselves for active duty on the First World War Front Line. Some 24,000 troops arrived and set themselves up in tented camps on and around Manor Farm. At the same time a Red Cross Hospital was set up near the church in Codford St Mary. The tented camps were soon converted into hutted sites and a total of fifteen camps were established in Codford, while nearby villages had a further twelve camps. The prime reason behind such an influx was the proximity of a railway station. Codford Station was on the Great Western Railway's Salisbury to Westbury branch. Soon after the tents were put up railway sidings were laid at Codford Station. But it was quickly realised that more rail facilities were needed and a line was laid to connect the different camps with the station. The line ran north of the station in an easterly direction, and then turned a half circle ending facing eastwards. The line then ran north of Codford St Peter to the north of Codford St Mary. A branch ran south alongside the hospital to end just to the east of the church in Codford St Mary. Three locomotives are recorded as having worked on the line; "Westminster" (also used at Bulford, Fargo and Fovant Camps), "Codford" (also used at Fovant Camp) and "Prince Edward".

In 1916 the camp was taken over by the New Zealand Command as a depot for wounded and sick men who had convalesced but were not yet ready for active service. This included the camp hospital, which had accommodation for 10 officers and 980 soldiers. In October 1918 there were nearly 3,500 troops stationed at the camp. Following the end of hostilities the troops went home and the camps were removed. It is assumed that the railway was removed at around the same time.

One lasting memorial of this time is the Australian Badge cut into the hillside of Lamb Down, just east of Codford St Mary. It was made in 1916 by defaulters from Sutton Veny Camp. 175 feet by 150 feet it originally had green, brown and clear beer bottles embedded in the shape, to give it a bronze colour in the sun, like the actual cap badges. Maintained by punishment parades it was given the name Misery Hill. Covered over during the Second World War to prevent enemy aircraft using it as a positioning aid, it was uncovered after the War, but most of the beer bottles had disappeared. So it is now a white badge, as the ground is chalk covered. On private land the badge is maintained annually by local villagers and Australian troops stationed in England as a monument to the Australian troops who fell during the two world wars. There is also an ANZAC War Grave Cemetery in Codford St Mary.

The area around Codford was used again in the Second World War for troop camps. However, the camps were on different sites and much less extensive than previously. There is no record of any railway being built during this period. The branch line serving Codford closed in the 1960s.

# FARGO MILITARY HOSPITAL

By the 1890s the breech loading cannon had become the weapon of choice by the Army. It was more powerful and more accurate than the earlier muzzle loading guns. For training and practice purposes large tracts of land were required. Initially a range was built at Oakhampton, Devon. Requirements soon outstripped the facilities and a further, larger, artillery range was set up at Larkhill on the Salisbury Plain, west of Amesbury. From 1900 many camps were built around Larkhill, including Knighton and Fargo. When the First World War began, the School of Gunnery moved to Larkhill. With a massive increase in the size of camps

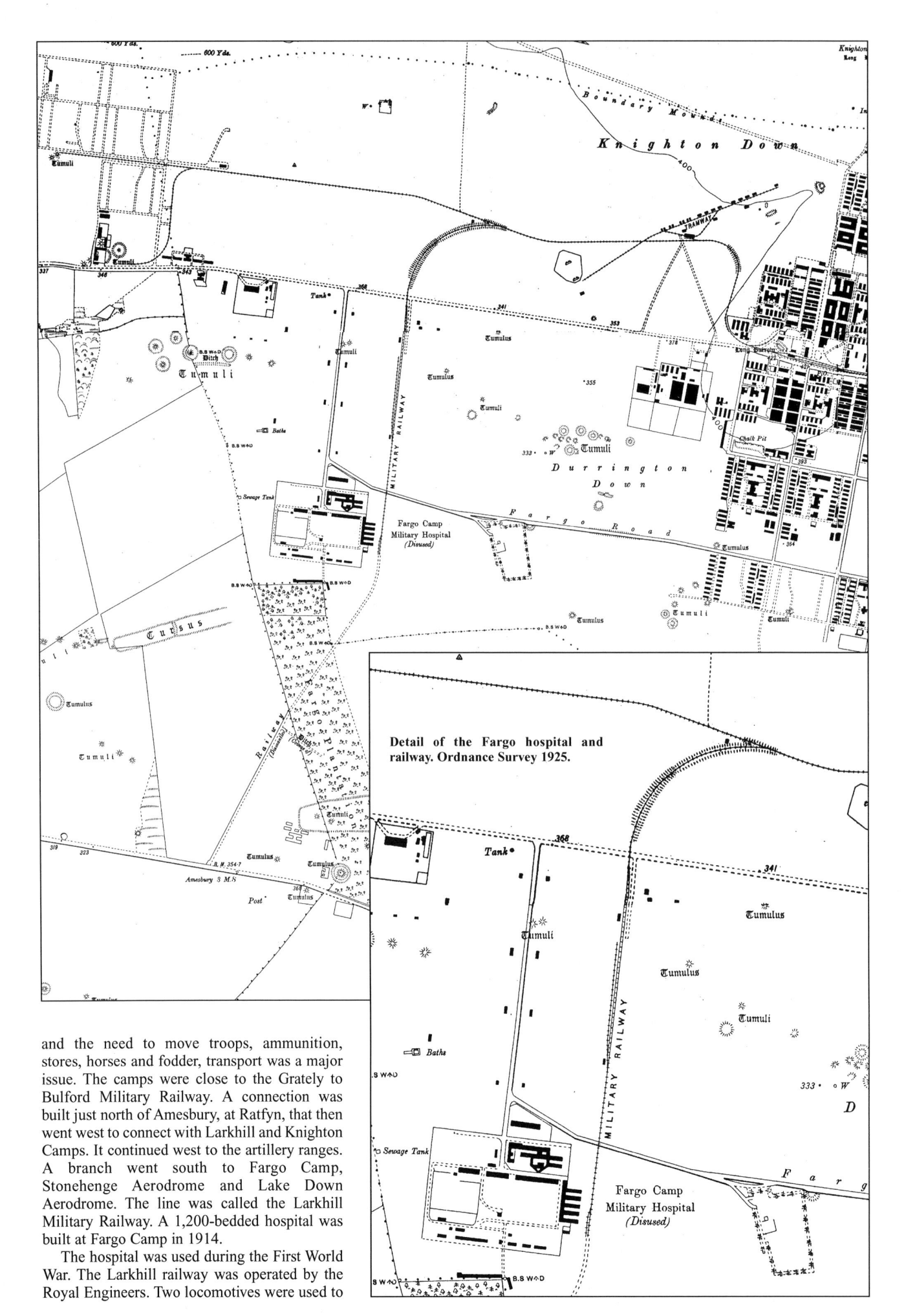

Detail of the Fargo hospital and railway. Ordnance Survey 1925.

and the need to move troops, ammunition, stores, horses and fodder, transport was a major issue. The camps were close to the Grately to Bulford Military Railway. A connection was built just north of Amesbury, at Ratfyn, that then went west to connect with Larkhill and Knighton Camps. It continued west to the artillery ranges. A branch went south to Fargo Camp, Stonehenge Aerodrome and Lake Down Aerodrome. The line was called the Larkhill Military Railway. A 1,200-bedded hospital was built at Fargo Camp in 1914.

The hospital was used during the First World War. The Larkhill railway was operated by the Royal Engineers. Two locomotives were used to

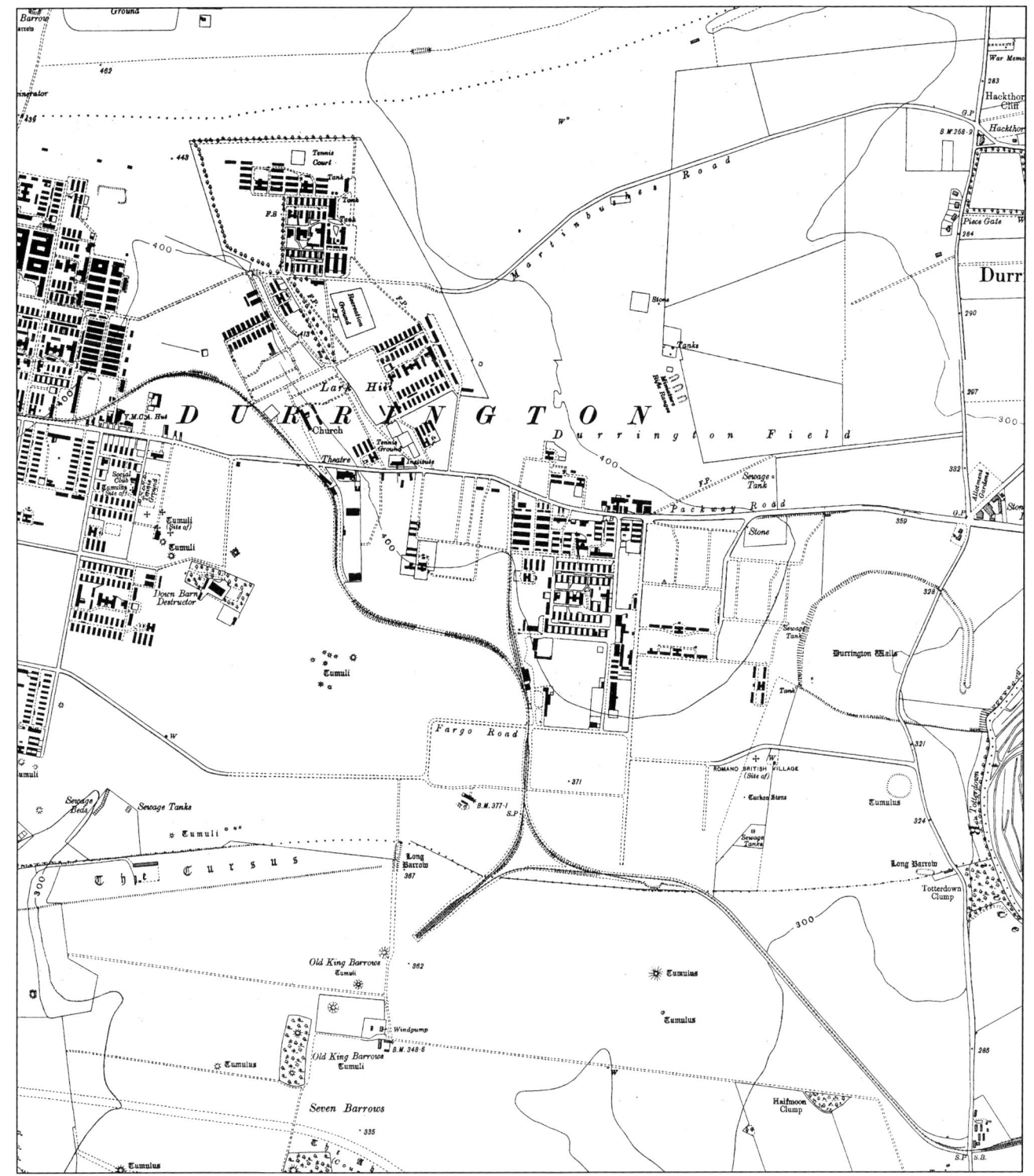

**Larkhill Military Railway with the branch to Fargo Hospital. Ordnance Survey 1925 and 1926.**

build the railway, an 0-4-0 saddle tank "Queen Mary" and an 0-6-0 side tank "Salisbury". They probably continued to be used on the line during the war and were joined for a short time by another 0-6-0 saddle tank, "Westminster", built by Peckett and at various times by "Bulford" (0-4-0 saddle tank), "Yorkshire", "Devonport" and "Chester" (all 0-6-0 tank engines)..

After the War the use declined and the hospital closed, with buildings being removed by around 1930. The railway closed in parts. The first to finish, in the early 1920s, were the branches to Stonehenge and Lake Down Aerodromes. The remainder of the Larkhill Military Railway closed in 1928 and the track removed by 1932.

**Built in 1914 for an order from the War Office "Westminster" is seen just after delivery to the Larkhill Military Railway, working to Fargo.**

# FOVANT CAMP MILITARY HOSPITAL

The villages of Fovant and Compton Chamberlayne are roughly eight miles west of Salisbury. Lying just south of the Salisbury Plain the rural tranquillity of the two villages was decimated in 1915 with the building of several army camps between and around the villages. In the following two years thousands of troops from over 30 different regiments and battalions spent time in the many camps. As well as the inevitable gunnery ranges, access roads and parade grounds, there was also a large hospital to treat wounded and sick soldiers, and a cinema for recreational time.

To provide the necessary supply of armament and provisions a 2½-mile rail link was made to Dinton Station. Dinton Station was owned by the London and South Western Railway (LSWR) and was on the Salisbury to Exeter main line. At the station there were exchange sidings and a platform. There was a further platform by the main camp, while the railway went further to a siding and ended alongside the hospital. The line opened on 15 October 1915. The map shows the rather convoluted route taken by the line. It starts with a semi-circle of track taking the train opposite the way it had started. Then a quarter circle took the line south to pass the village of Fovant on its eastern side. Then another quarter circle took it eastwards towards Compton Chamberlayne, finishing about half way between the villages and alongside the camp hospital. The tight curves and a gradient of 1 in 35 meant that the small locomotives used on the line were given a hard test each time they hauled a train up the hill.

The Camp hospital was sited in a separate field to the main camp. It opened soon after the first troops arrived in October 1915, with 150 beds and grew in size, as demands on its services increased, to around 600 beds. The hospital comprised both wooden huts and tented accommodation. The military railway was used to convey ambulance trains from the south coast docks directly to the hospital site. The hospital itself had the usual military doctors and nurses, but more staff were needed and local villagers, including the GP, were asked to work, tending to the wounded

At the end of the War the camp was no longer needed. However, it was not until 1921 that demolition of the camp began, a process that would go on for three years. The railway was used to transport materials from the camps. The railway line was last used in February 1924 and the rails were lifted in 1926. Although the hospital closed nearly ninety years ago the site is still known as Hospital Field.

The railway had its own locomotives. Like many of the military railways around Salisbury the line had some ancient locomotives. There were two such at Fovant, an 1878 4-4-0 tank locomotive and an 1882 4-4-2 tank engine. In addition the line

**A view across Fovant Camp during the First World War, the railway runs from the middle of the clump of trees on the left in a horizontal line across the photograph. Hospital Field is on the right above the line of the railway.**

**The station at Fovant Camp with one of the locomotives used on the line. The train in the photograph was used for troop movements and is not an ambulance train.**

had three other locomotives, "Westminster", "Seafield" an 0-6-0 saddle tank built in 1914 and "Codford" an 0-4-0 saddle tank built in 1905. The history of "Westminster" is well documented, an 0-6-0 saddle tank locomotive, it was built in 1914 by Peckett and Sons. It was originally allocated to the Bulford Camp Military Railway but it was moved in 1917 to Fovant where it stayed for the duration. Its life after the closing of the Fovant line in 1924 is not recorded until it was purchased by the Associated Portland Cement Company (APCC) in the 1960s. Later it was sold into private ownership including the Kent and East Sussex Railway. In 1998 it was discovered on a short length of private track at the old station at East Tisted. The Northampton and Lamport Railway, a preserved line, purchased the locomotive in 1998. It is currently under extensive restoration.

Like many of the camps around Salisbury Plain the soldiers used some of their time (often as punishment duty) to cut representations of their cap badges into hillsides around the area. Nine of these badges are still visible. In the 1950s the Fovant Home Guard Old Comrades Association restored the visible badges and added their own, the Wiltshire Regiment, and the Royal Wiltshire Yeomanry. With reducing numbers of Home Guard Old Comrades the Fovant Badges Society (a registered charity) was established that continues to maintain the badges. In 1970 the badge of the Royal Corps of Signals was added and together with the badges of the 7th Battalion (City of London) Regiment, and the Royal Warwickshire Regiment, at Sutton Mandeville, there are now twelve badges cut in the hillside.

Traces of the track bed of the old railway are still visible around Fovant – mainly embankments and cuttings. Parts of the line are now used as public footpaths.

**"Westminster" in the 1970s when it was owned by the Associated Portland Cement Company. Photograph Roger Monk.**

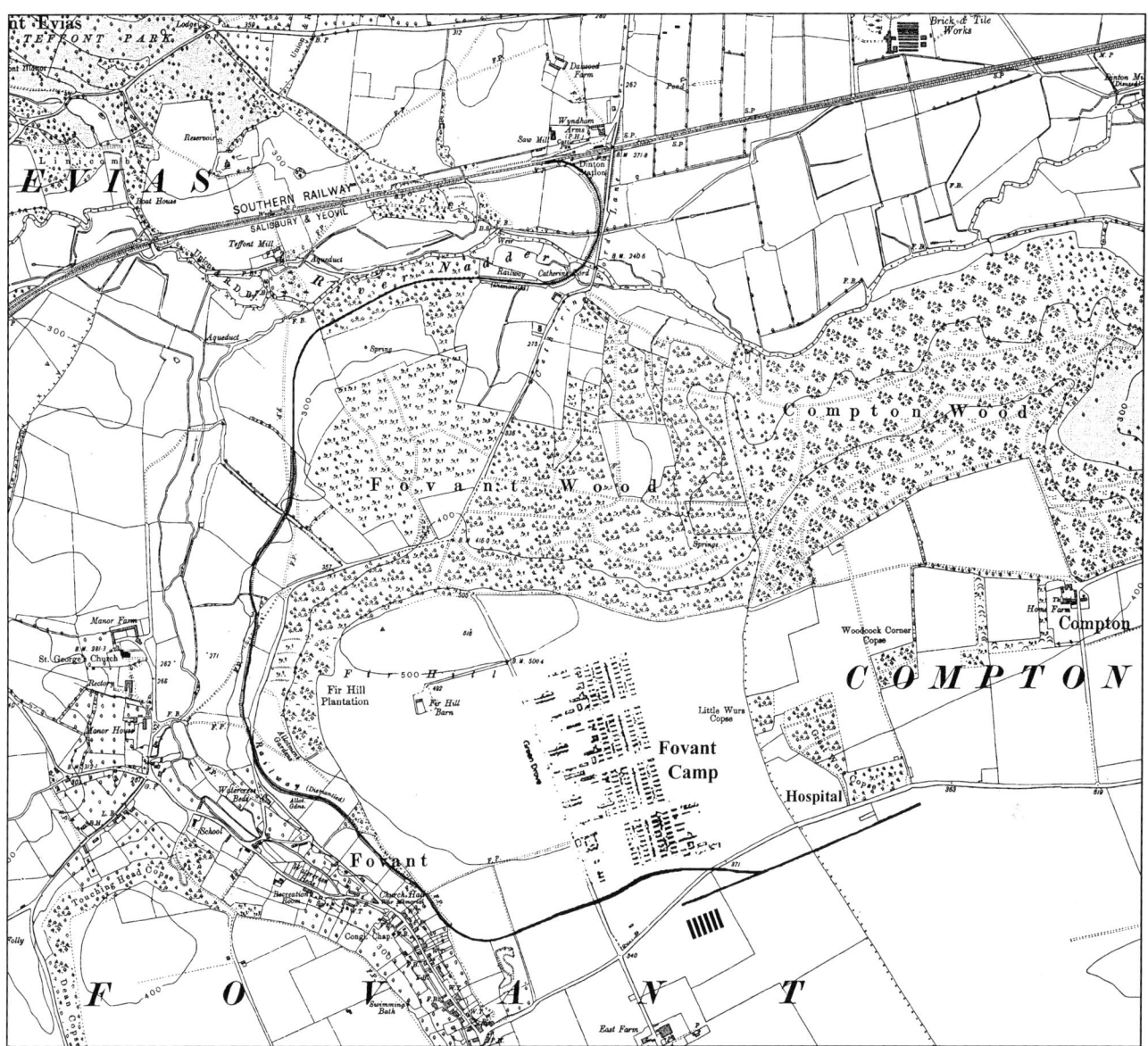

**Fovant Camp railway superimposed onto the Ordnance Survey Map 1925.**

# INGRESS ABBEY MILITARY HOSPITAL

Standing on the edge of the Thames at Greenhithe the history of the Ingress Abbey estate goes back to the 12th Century, when Edward III endowed the estate to the Prioress and Abbey of Dartford. It was subsequently owned by various people until in the 1850s the War Office recognised that there was a need for pre-sea training for potential officers in the Royal and Merchant Navy. The Thames Nautical Training College was set up by a group of London ship owners. The Admiralty loaned a ship HMS Worcester which was moored at Blackwall Reach. The ship was moved to several different places before finding a permanent home at the jetty by Ingress Abbey Greenhithe. Over the years the ships were changed, but the name was always HMS Worcester. Land and buildings at Ingress Abbey were purchased as land based training facilities to complement the ship.

In 1908 a paper mill, called Ingress Abbey Paper Mills, was built to the east of Ingress Abbey and slightly nearer to the river. As part of the development a private railway line was built to connect the paper mill with a wharf and with the South Eastern & Chatham Railway (SECR) by Greenhithe Station. Given the dangers of fire in the paper mills they purchased the first fireless steam locomotive to run in Britain, that was built for them by Orenstein and Koppel, Germany. The railway line ran along the western and northern boarders of the Abbey grounds.

As Ingress Abbey was owned by the armed forces it was used during the First World War as a hospital. Advantage was taken of the private siding running alongside the Abbey's grounds. Around 1915 a wooden platform was constructed near to the Abbey to allow wounded soldiers to be brought by rail to the

**Ingress Abbey when it was used as a naval training establishment.**

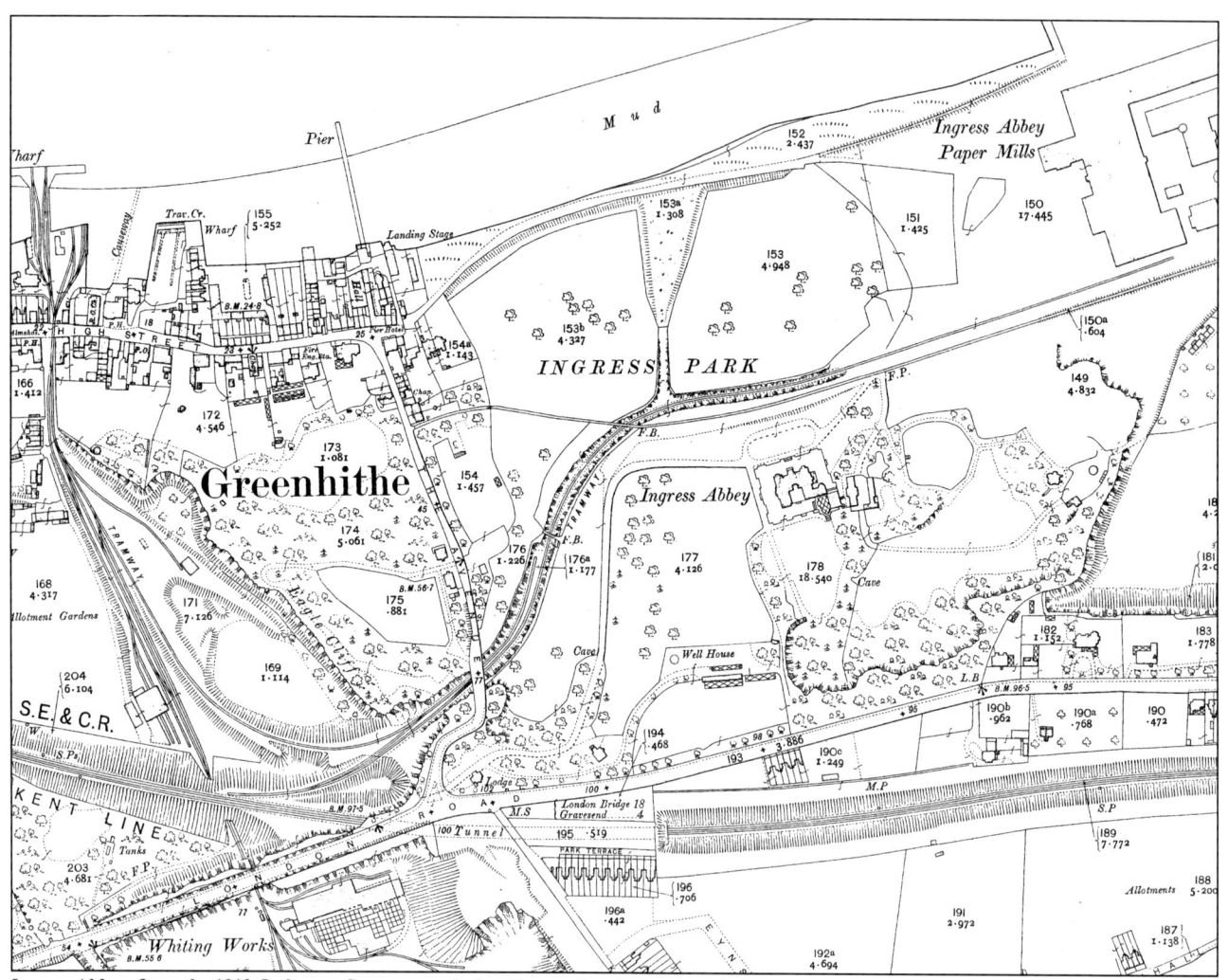

**Ingress Abbey, from the 1910 Ordnance Survey map, before the wooden platform was built.**

hospital. Information is extremely sketchy and the precise location of the platform is not known. Quite possibly the platform was directly in front of the Abbey buildings. The directions for railway staff using the siding were "Enginemen are to proceed cautiously from the time they enter Ingress Park siding until they arrive at Ingress Abbey Platform. Locomotive Department to arrange for a Backing-on Engine to be provided at Greenhithe to haul the Loaded Trains into the Siding when arriving on the Up Line, or hauling the empty Ambulance Trains up the bank into Greenhithe when the loaded train arrives in the Down direction."

The Abbey remained as a temporary hospital until 1918, when it returned to its training duties. By 1926, when the Ordnance Survey revised their maps, the platform had been removed and no trace is shown on the map.

A brand new training establishment was built in 1974/75 in the grounds of the Abbey and Park. The private railway was still being used by the paper mills and one

**Ingress Abbey from the 1928 Ordnance Survey map. The private railway linking the SECR main line to the paper mills is clearly shown. The private line also linked the mills with the wharf and a chalk pit.**

52

of the college buildings was built bridging the railway line. Strangely the College did not last much longer as, despite the new facilities, the college closed in 1989. The buildings stood until 1999 when they were demolished to make way for a housing estate. Ingress Abbey itself was threatened, but after a successful campaign the buildings and part of the historic park has been restored and incorporated into a large riverside housing development.

Ingress Abbey from the air. The new buildings are all part of the college. Note the largest building has been built over the private railway line. The course of the railway is easily seen in the cutting.

# MORLEY US MILITARY HOSPITAL

Morley Hall and its extensive grounds are about twelve miles south west of Norwich, close to the town of Wymondham. After the First World War the grounds were made into links by the Mid-Norfolk Golf Club. However, in 1939 the land was requisitioned by the War Office for agricultural use. Then in 1943 it was decided that a military hospital should be built on the land. So a complex of corrugated iron Nissen huts, brick buildings and wooden huts were built that became the 77th Station Hospital of the US Army. Most of the patients were air crew casualties during the heavy bomber raids over Germany.

Then in 1944 the 231st Station Hospital moved from Diss to Morley Park and the hospital at Wymondham was renamed the 231st. Whilst continuing to care for the flying personnel, the hospital also received casualties from the D-Day offensive, expanding the number of beds from 834 to 1254. These were put in tents erected between the Nissen huts. While the aircrew patients would be taken by ambulance from the airfields to the hospital, the casualties arriving from France were brought by train. The hospital was close to the London and North Eastern Railway's Norwich to Cambridge line, so D-Day casualties were

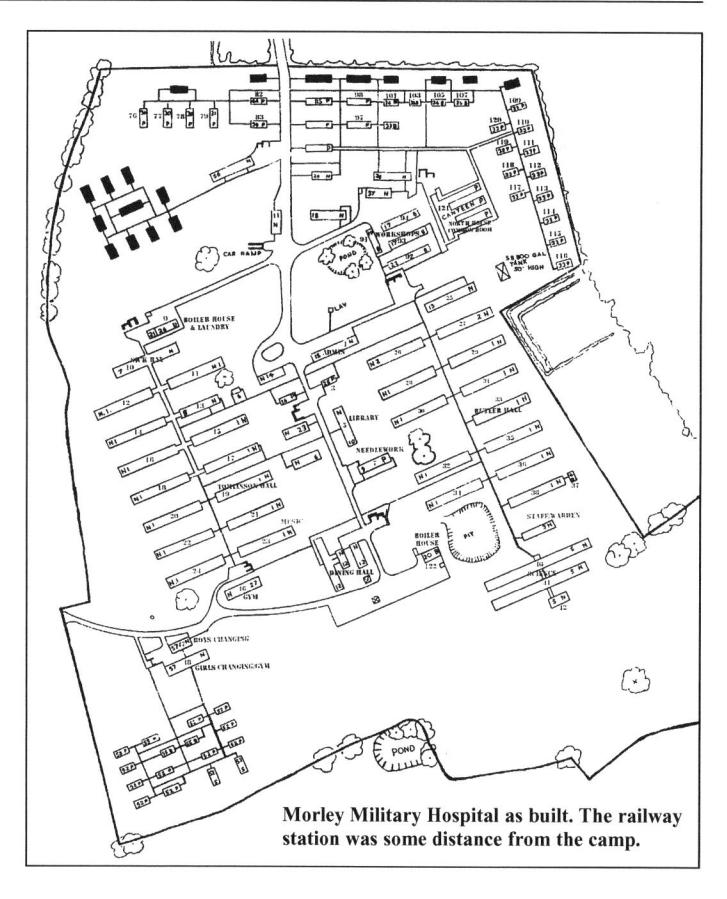

Morley Military Hospital as built. The railway station was some distance from the camp.

53

**Morley Military Hospital used by United States troops during the Second World War. The railway did not actually enter the camp grounds.**

taken by Hospital train to Wymondham Railway Station. Here they were taken on stretchers by ambulance to the hospital. In the last half of 1944 over 2,000 patients were brought by eight hospital trains and over 1,000 in 1945. About a third of the patients needed orthopaedic treatment. Like most US military hospitals in this country it had a prisoner of war camp attached to it.

The hospital closed in 1945 and the Ministry of Works began converting the camp into two emergency colleges to train ex-servicemen and women who wished to qualify as teachers, as there was a national shortage. One college was exclusively for men the other for women. The last training college students left in December 1950. The site was then taken over by Wymondham College, a state boarding school for boys and girls aged between 11 and 18 years of age. It is now one of only two state boarding schools in the country.

Wymondham Station continues to serve the community. Indeed it reached the finals of the "Small Station of the Year" National Rail Awards in 2002, 2003 and 2004. This is well deserved as the station is immensely attractive with a profusion of flowers in a completely litter free station. There is also a small museum of railway memorabilia on the Westbound platform.

**Wymondham Station in the 1940s, looking the same as it did when used by the US troops.**

# SUTTON VENY MILITARY HOSPITAL

Sutton Veny is a small village two to three miles south east of Warminster and not far from Salisbury Plain and within easy travelling of the south coast ports. In the First World War it was a good choice for an army camp for soldiers about to go to the Western Front to fight. In fact there were around ten camps in the area. The Sutton Veny Camp was set up in 1914 with a three

**This photograph shows how much of an impact Veny Camp must have had on the small rural hamlet.**

**Sutton Veny Camp after the wooden huts had been established. The railway runs between the huts and the tented area.**

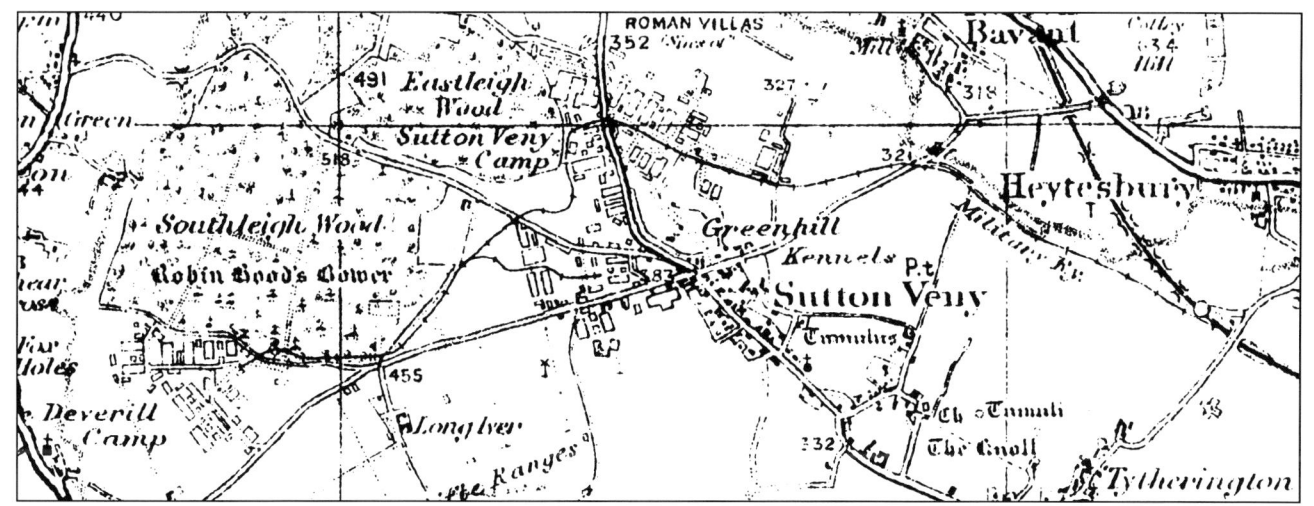

Sutton Veny camp showing the position of the hospital and the line of the railway. Ordnance Survey one inch map of 1915.

and a half mile railway link being built from Heytesbury Station, on the Great Western Railway's Salisbury to Westbury line, into the camp itself. The work was carried out by hundreds of navvies who had descended on the village living in huts, tents or out rough. The railway carried supplies and troops to and from the camp. A two-foot gauge contractor's railway was also built during the construction of the camp. This was then used to distribute supplies from the main railhead to the other camps. Initially the camp was used for training purposes, the first troops arriving in 1915. Practice trenches had been built where the troops would spend a week getting used to conditions that they would soon have as permanent accommodation.

In 1916 a Hospital Camp was built between Bishopstraw and Sutton Veny to tend for war wounded. The hospital was built alongside the railway so that wounded troops could be taken from the ambulance trains straight into the reception centre and then on to the wards. A prisoner of war camp was also built in Sutton Veny. Some of the first casualties to be treated were wounded German Prisoners of War. They had an angry reception from the women of the village, who threatened to lynch them.

Then in 1918 the No 1 Australian General Hospital was moved to Sutton Veny Camp where it stayed until 1919. Many of the troops succumbed to the virulent influenza that spread amongst the soldiers in 1918 and killed thousands. Eventually the Australians returned home and the railway was lifted. Greenhill House (now Sutton Veny House) was a rest and recuperation centre run by the Australian YMCA for the troops.

During the Second World War two camps were opened in Sutton Veny, including a military hospital. These camps were far smaller than the previous ones. There is no record of the rail link being re-established.

The village still commemorates ANZAC Day every year, with an ANZAC Memorial Chapel in the local church, St John the Evangelist. Sutton Veny House is now a nursing home. The railway line from Salisbury to Westbury is still open but Heytesbury Station no longer exists, having closed some years ago.

One of the locomotives used on the Sutton Veny line.

The railway in Sutton Veny Camp. The narrow gauge railway was used to distribute supplies throughout the camp. The temporary feel of the camp is because the photograph was taken during construction, so there are piles of wood around and the track has been laid very quickly.

# TIDWORTH CAMP MILITARY HOSPITAL

In 1879 the War Office purchased Tedworth House and the adjoining estate. This was to be the beginnings of the vast Salisbury Plain complex of military camps and training areas. The first camp to be erected was Tidworth, some twelve miles west of Salisbury. The camp covered 460 acres and building was started in 1901. As part of the development the War office commissioned the building of a railway from Ludgershall Station, on the Midland and South Western Junction Railway, to Tidworth, with the aim of providing a rail service to the camp. A station was built at Tidworth and the line continued into the camp. It was used to carry men and materials for the construction of the camp. As a very large workforce was needed, temporary accommodation was built between Tidworth and Ludgershall, which became known as "Tin Town". The contractor was granted permission to put a siding at the camp to enable the men to be transported to the building site. The line from Ludgershall to Tidworth was owned by the War Department, but operated under contract by the Midland and South Western Junction Railway. The line within the camp was operated by military personnel.

The camp was opened in 1904, with some building work still to be completed. The camp did not have a hospital for the soldiers, but it did have a Station Veterinary Hospital, to care for the horses that were the power providers at that time. An isolation hospital had been built at Brimstone Bottom, but this did not provide general medical care for the troops. As the camp became more occupied it was clear that hospital facilities were needed. So in 1907 some of the barracks buildings (Delhi barracks) were converted to a 120-bedded Military Hospital. It was very close to the camp railway.

The railway was very busy, carrying supplies for the barracks. In addition to military materials there was also a vast amount of provisions needed by the men. For example there were three full wagons of flour every week. All the coal for the barracks was brought in by rail. The volume was such that each of the eight barrack units had its own coal yard. With troops travelling to and from the camp on leave and having visits from family members the annual receipts for

**"Betty" one of the locomotives that worked on the Tidworth Railway accompanied by her driver, fireman and shunters.**

**Another of the locomotives that worked on the Tidworth Military Railway.**

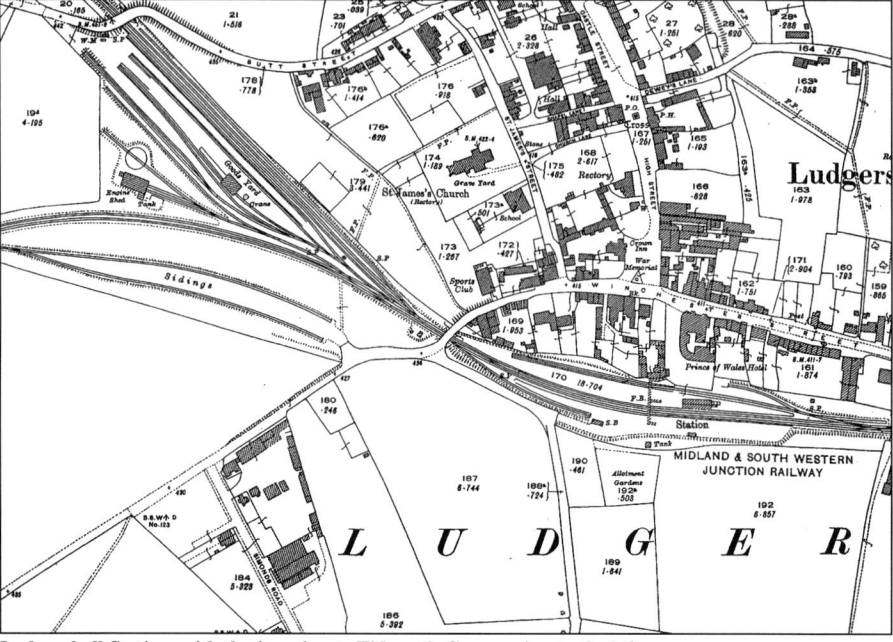

**Ludgershall Station, with the junction to Tidworth Camp going to the left.**

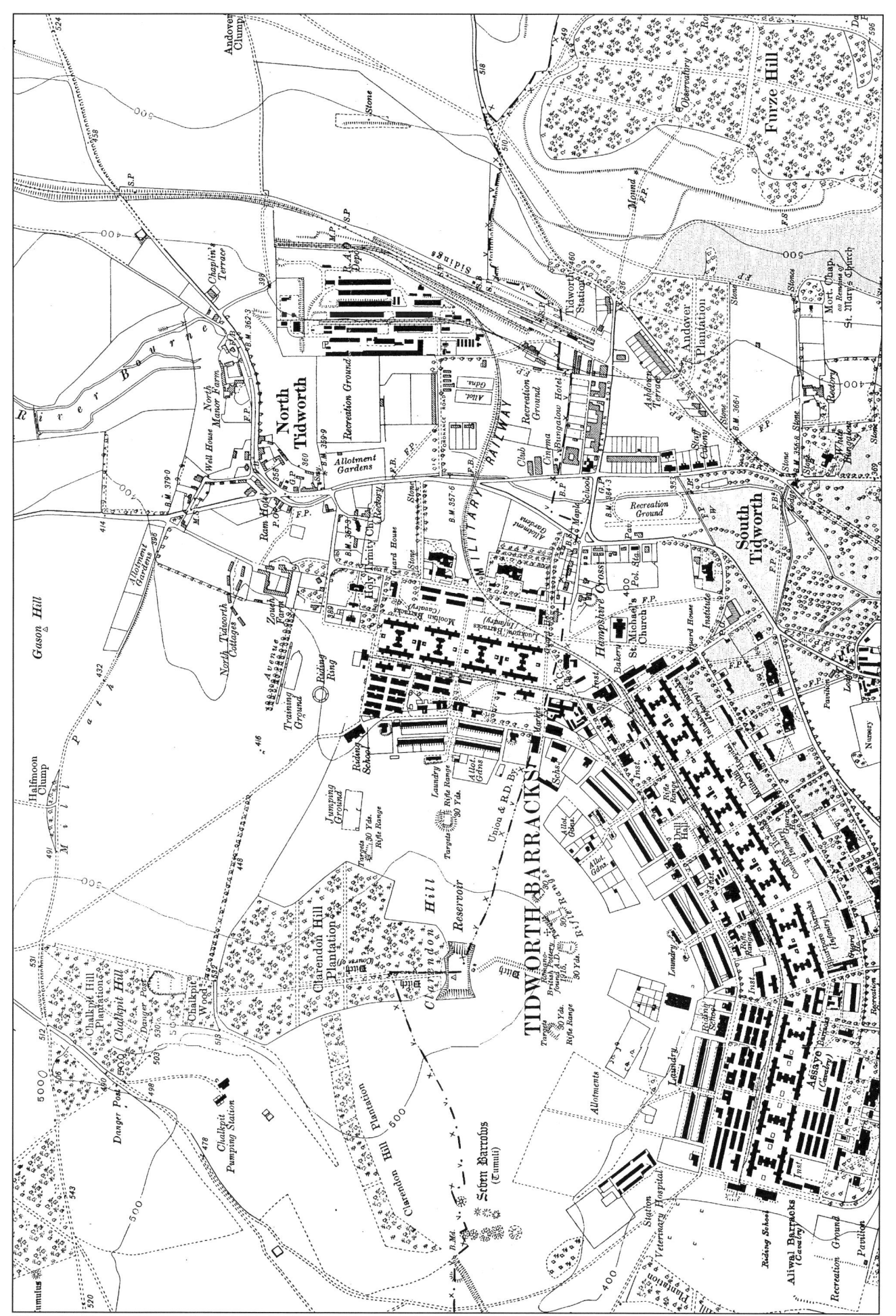

**Tidworth military railway and camp, with the sidings to the Royal Ordnance Depot.**

Scorning the luxuries of passenger carriages the workmen building Tidworth Camp travel to the site by open wagon.

All the excavation had to be carried out by hand, with just picks and shovels.

A winter scene showing Tidworth Station with a special run for relatives of the wounded soldiers.

Tidworth Station were greater than all the other stations of the Midland and South Western Junction Railway put together.

Like all the camps on the Salisbury Plain, Tidworth became extremely busy during the First World War, with troops congregating there prior to going overseas. This was also a busy period for the railway. In 1914 a locomotive was requisitioned from the Bute Works Supply Company Ltd. Built in 1862 by Manning Wardle of Leeds the 0-6-0 saddle tank locomotive had worked on several different industrial railways. Painted in a blue and white scheme it was given the name "Hecate". Wounded troops were transported by rail from the south coast docks to the hospital at Tidworth. Nearly 1,500 ambulance trains were run over the line. Given the close proximity of the camp railway to the hospital it is likely that some of the wounded were taken into the camp by rail. The more ambulant casualties would have transferred at Tidworth station and walked to the hospital.

The locomotive was given a new boiler in 1916. It continued to operate until 1928 when it was abandoned on a siding at Tidworth Station and sold for scrap in 1929. At this time two new locomotives arrived, an 0-6-0 saddle tank called "Betty"

Ludgershall Station during the First World War with a train load of horses being unloaded by the troops.

and an 0-4-0 Sentinel called "Molly" of the LNER Y6 design. During the Second World War an 0-6-0 saddle tank locomotive was borrowed. However, this proved too heavy for the bridge over the Salisbury Road and could only work to the Royal Artillery Ordinance Depot (RAOD). In 1942 the camp was occupied by the US Army. They brought their own 0-6-0 locomotives that were used on the Ludgershall sidings. There are no records of whether Tidford Military Hospital was used extensively for wounded troops in the Second World War. No doubt the railway was busy with troop movements and for transporting ordinance to the camp. However, it is not possible to determine if the railway was used for hospital trains. There is a photograph of Tidworth Station with a row of ambulances along the platform which suggests that it was used for wounded troops. After the War "Molly" and "Betty" were in bad repair and so were sold and went to the Channel Islands. They were replaced with two 0-4-0 saddle tank locomotives. In the early 1950s the bridge over the road was condemned and the line to the barracks was closed. Only the line to the RAOD remained open. This allowed the two 0-4-0 locomotives to be replaced by an 0-6-0 saddle tank called "Woolmer". This did not last long, being sent to the Longmoor Military Railway. Two Austerity 0-6-0 saddle tank engines were acquired, but there was little work for them to do. So they were transferred to Shoeburyness and a Gardner's diesel locomotive was used. In 1955 the working of the Ludgershall to Tidworth branch was taken over by the military and it was known as the Tidworth Ludgershall Military Railway. It was operated on the one engine in steam principle.

In 1953 the RAOD closed and with it the purpose of the line. So it too closed and the track was lifted soon after. In Tidworth Camp the hospital closed in 1977.

**Tidworth Station in the early days. The connection to the Camp is just beyond the signal box (in the right distance) and goes to the left of the photograph.**

**Tidworth Station between the Wars. The connection to the Camp is where the trucks are by the signals.**

**Tidworth Camp with the railway running through the site.**

**To us it is surprising how much horse movement was carried out by the railways. The wide platform at Ludgershall was very useful for such activity.**

**Tidworth Station, the rail connection to the Camp is a short distance before the station.**

59

# SCOTTISH HOSPITAL TRAMWAYS AND RAILWAYS

Among the first asylums to be built in Scotland were seven opened between 1722 and 1857 under the auspices of Royal Charters. Managed by Asylum Boards the hospitals were located close to cities and large towns. The asylums were intended to provide treatment for the poor of the community, then called pauper lunatics. The way that these people were treated became to be seen as a public disgrace and this led in 1857 to the Scottish Lunacy Act. This set standards of care for the patients that all asylums had to meet. There was also an emphasis on prevention as well as treatment. Until the passing of the Act the main aim of the asylums was to keep costs as low as possible. This included taking in private patients, who were paid for by their families and who subsidised the running of the whole asylum.

The Act also set up a Board of Control who was to monitor the activities of the local District Lunacy Boards.

## BANGOUR HOSPITAL

*Also known as:*
**Bangour Asylum**
**Edinburgh War Hospital**

In the 1890s Edinburgh was finding it did not have sufficient care facilities for its pauper lunatics. The Edinburgh District Lunacy Board decided that the solution was to purchase land at Bangour, near Broxburn some 14 miles west of Edinburgh. Such was the need for more accommodation the initial buildings were hurriedly constructed and the first patients moved in during 1904, while the hospital itself was not officially opened until 1906. The complex included a large reservoir to ensure a regular water supply to the hospital. The one and a half miles long railway was built to take materials to the building site and part of the contract was that the section from Dechmont station to the hospital should then transfer as a private railway to the hospital, while the line from Uphall to Dechmont would be operated by the North British Railway (NBR) as a public railway. The NBR took over the running of the line from 1904, possibly including relaying the track. The infrastructure, such as station buildings were built over the next twelve months. This may have been to allow the contractor's railway to continue to operate as the hospital was still being built. The line was inspected and opened for general use in 1905.

Trains for the hospital would start from Uphall station, travel half a mile along the NBR line to the junction and then take the

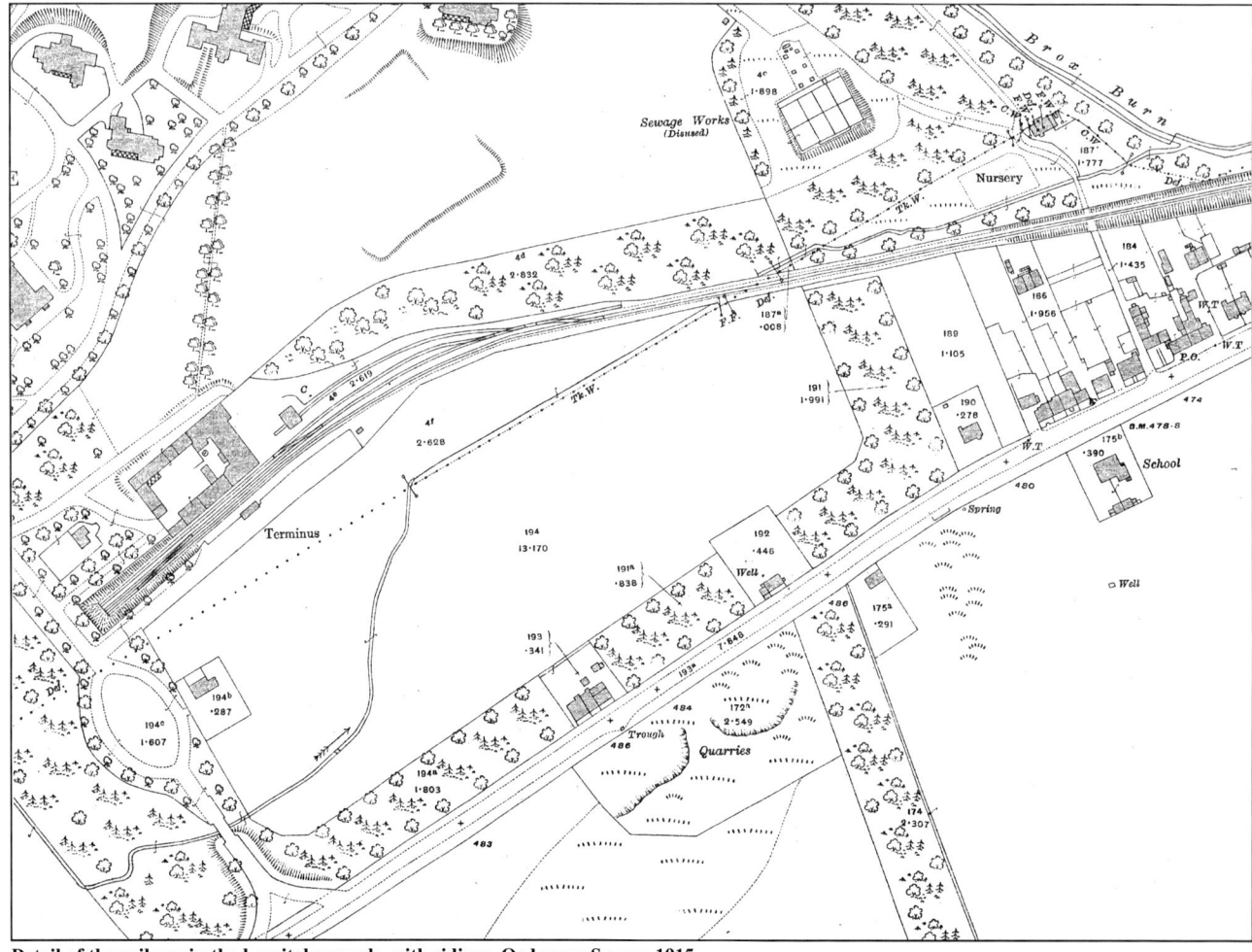

**Detail of the railway in the hospital grounds, with sidings. Ordnance Survey 1915.**

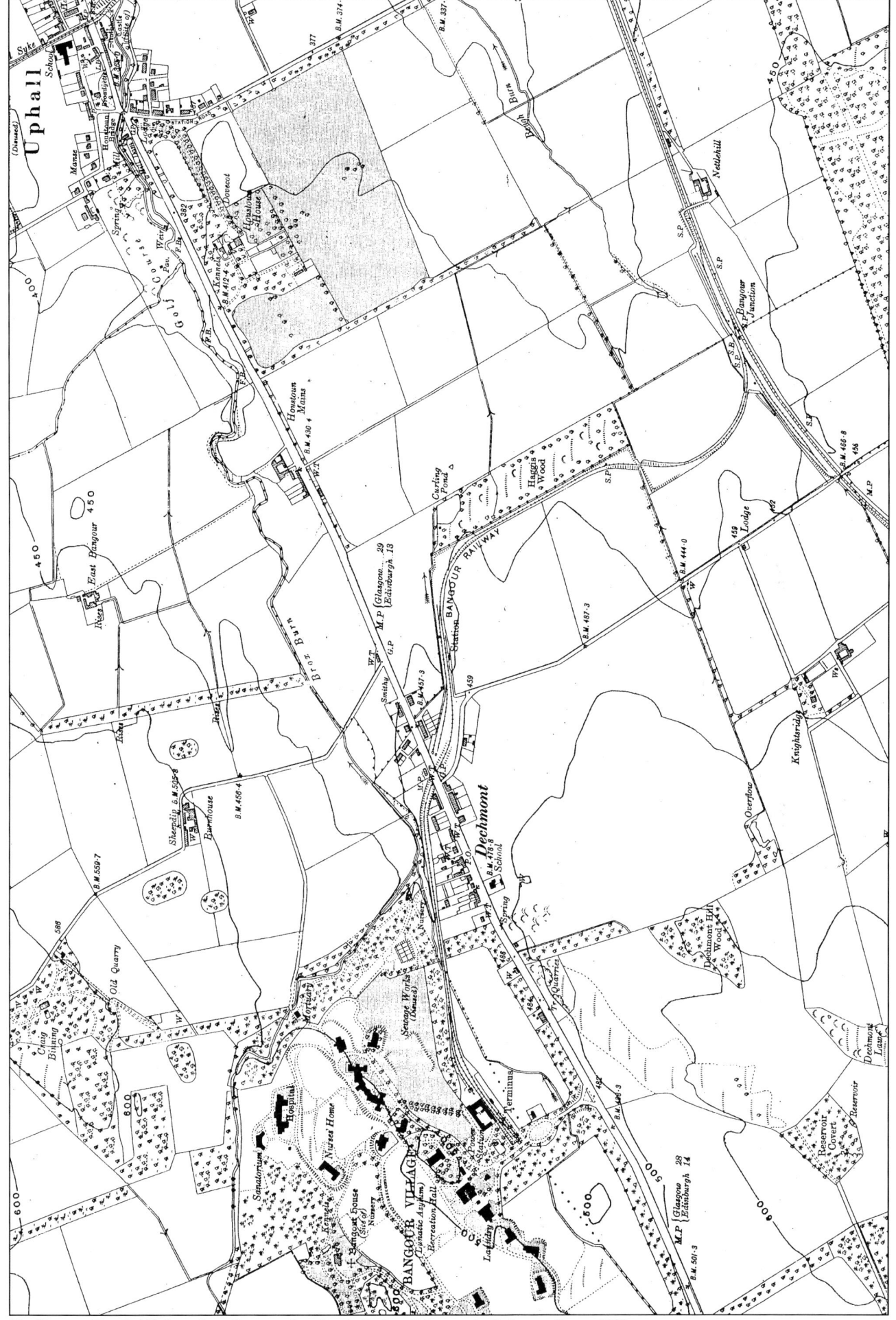

**The Bangour Hospital Railway from Bangour Junction to the hospital grounds. Ordnance Survey 1922.**

**Early photograph of Bangour Hospital platform. The hospital boiler house is on the left.**

**Bangour Hospital platform during the First World War, with wounded soldiers being moved from the ambulance train to the wards.**

**Another early view, in the opposite direction with the hospital buildings on the right behind the train.**

branch line to Dechmont and Bangour. Dechmont was a single platform halt. The line then ran into the hospital grounds to a terminus platform named Bangour (Private). There was a run-round loop and a further siding that was used by the coal wagons unloading at the boiler house. Only one locomotive at a time was allowed on the branch line, so no signalling was necessary away from the junction. Passenger trains usually consisted of three small carriages hauled by a Drummond 4-4-0 tank engine. Three passenger trains were scheduled each day, except Sundays when no trains were run. There was also one daily goods train.

In 1915 the hospital was requisitioned by the War Office as a military hospital. Patients were transferred to other hospitals around the country. It now cared for war wounded troops. The soldiers would arrive by ship in Southampton and then be taken by ambulance train to Bangour. The trains could be as long as twelve coaches and were taken all the way to the platform at Bangour. Here an ambulance shed had been erected to enable the transfer of patients from the trains to the wards. Additional beds had been added in tented accommodation. The hospital treated 45,000 wounded soldiers during the war. At maximum the hospital could take 3,000 patients at any one time.

Returning the hospital to its old role after the war took a while. The last of the transferred patients did not return until 1922. During this period it became evident that improvements in road transport were taking most of the traffic off the branch line. So the hospital authorities decided to close the line on July 31st 1921. The track was lifted soon after.

The hospital was again requisitioned in 1939 for the Second World War, becoming the Edinburgh War Hospital, but there were no proposals to relay the line and all patients arrived in ambulances by road. An annex was built at this time that was called Bangour General Hospital. The General Hospital continued until the early 1990s when the work was transferred to more modern facilities and the Bangour General hospital closed.

In 2004 the hospital was thrust into the public eye when the film "The Jacket" was filmed in the grounds. The executive producer of the £20 million film was George Clooney. The hospital itself has now closed and the site is likely to be used for housing development.

# DYKEBAR HOSPITAL

*Also known as:*
**Renfrew District Lunatic Asylum**

In the early 1900s the Renfrew District Lunacy Board decided to build a new hospital for pauper lunatics. The site chosen was two miles south east of the centre of Paisley. Designed by the foremost Paisley architect of the time, T.G. Abercrombie, Dykebar Hospital was built in 1909. In the grounds of the hospital a large house, called Mid Dykebar, was erected at the same time for the use of the Hospital Superintendent.

The land that the hospital was built on was effectively surrounded by railways. The Paisley and Barrhead District Railway (built in 1897, becoming part of the Caledonian Railway in 1902) ran alongside the hospital. The Hospital Board made use of this facility and connection was laid from the hospital to the railway line. It consisted of a single track siding running from the main line across the hospital site to the laundry and boiler house.

In 1916 the hospital was requisitioned by the War Department and became Dykebar War Hospital with 500 beds for soldiers suffering from mental illness. It continued to be used by the military until 1919 when it reverted back to a civilian mental hospital. There is no record of the railway having been used to transport soldiers to the hospital. It is probable that the hospital railway was only used for goods work. It appears to have been worked by the main line trains. Goods trains would leave Paisley and deliver coal to the hospital and then carry on to take more coal to Barrhead Gasworks and to Thomas McDonald Ltd at Barrhead Station. The same trains would also take tar tankers to the Dussick & Bitumen Company and malt waste (draff) from breweries to West Arthurlie Farm for cattle feed.

In 1936 there was a severe fire in the administrative block causing £7,000-worth of damage, an enormous sum in those days.

**Mid Dykebar House, showing its deterioration, despite being listed.**

Along with most other hospitals in Scotland it joined the National Health Service in 1948. It became part of the Renfrewshire Mental Hospitals Board of Management (renamed the Dykebar and Associated Hospitals Board of Management in 1964). From 1968 to 1974 it was part of the Paisley and District Hospitals Board of Management. At the re-organisation of 1974 it passed to the Renfrew District of the new Argyll and Clyde Health Board. Around this time a completely new hospital was built on the site.

The superintendent's house, Mid Dykebar, was listed in 1992. However, it has been allowed to deteriorate and has been attacked by vandals.

The Paisley and Barrhead branch closed in 1981 and the rails were lifted in 1987. The date of the final use of the hospital siding is not known, but was probably soon after the war.

In 2004 the hospital was selected as the site for the secure care centre for the whole of the west of Scotland. It will be used for mentally ill patients requiring a greater level of security than those in conventional psychiatric hospitals.

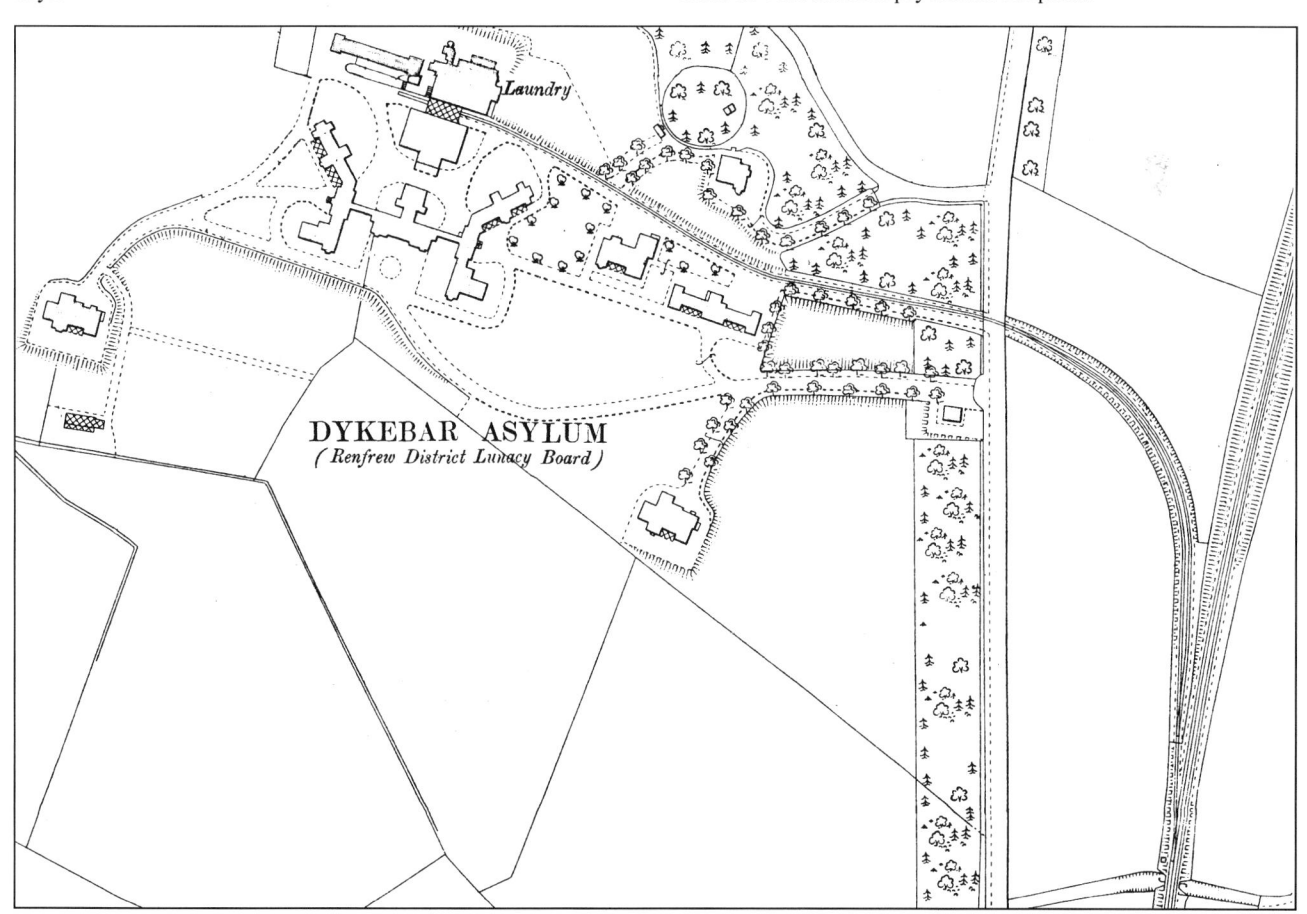

**The Dykebar Hospital Railway. Ordnance Survey 1912.**

# GLASGOW ROYAL INFIRMARY

I am indebted to Dr I.D.O. Frew for readily agreeing to my using his article on the unusual accumulator railway that ran underground at Glasgow Royal Infirmary. The hospital had been originally built in 1794 with 136 beds. It was extended in the 19th Century. As demands on its services extended plans were drawn up for a massive reconstruction and this took place between 1909 and 1914. This was when the underground railway was constructed.

The article reproduced below was first published in the June 1972 issue of Scottish Transport, the magazine of the Scottish Tramway and Transport Society.

## THE GLASGOW ROYAL INFIRMARY RAILWAY

Glasgow's First Electrically Operated "Underground" Railway by Dr I.D.O. Frew

In the early years of the century a massive reconstruction scheme was undertaken, modernising and enlarging one of Scotland's most ancient and famous medical institutions. The magnificently graceful building by Robert and James Adam standing on the site of the Archbishop's Palace was swept away without a murmur of protest and an ugly three-winged monstrosity erected in stages in its place. Though unbeautiful, every effort was made to make the new hospital as up-to-date and efficient as possible and the handling of the laundry was entrusted to a specially designed electric railway. The laundry lay in a building somewhat behind and below the three ward wings and the railway ran totally in buildings or tunnel.

The line started in fact in the boiler house where loco maintenance was undertaken, and from there was a 135-foot section of line used for wagon storage. At this point the line ran alongside the laundry entrance and here the previously level route began a 265-foot long 1-in-10 climb at the top of which was the surgical block. Halfway up the gradient the line executed a distinctly sharp double wiggle taking the line around the corner of the nurses' home.

From the top of the gradient the line ran in the sub-basement of the new hospital, the section to the surgical wing being opened in 1908. A siding ran off to the surgical lifts and the main route turned sharply at right angles running straight for 400 feet sending off a short siding at the centre block lifts half way along. A further right angled turn took the line to its terminus at the medical block lifts. At the surgical lifts the sub-basement has a 12-foot headroom, but this decreases steadily to only 5 feet at its terminus. The extension to the centre block opened in 1912 and the last section in 1914.

To work the line a battery electric loco was constructed by Malcolm and Allen Ltd, of Eglinton Street, Glasgow—the only loco ever built by this firm which now operates in the motor trade. This machine was in effect a four-wheeled platform carrying a box which held the batteries, motor, and controls. The entire machine measured 5' 6" long, 4' 0" wide, and 4' 0" high. The wagons were all steel and the body formed from plates rivetted together, measuring 6' 2" long, 2' 6" broad, and 2' 4" high. There were 4 cast wheels at 2' 6" centres each bearing the inscription "Hamilton & Sons, Glasgow". The track was just 2' 3" gauge and the rails were "L" shaped bars cemented into place with only occasional metal ties. Unhappily the line was not a success. The batteries ran down continually and the equipment appears to have been more than a little primitive. The loco was very noisy in use, particularly in the more confined areas of operation, and on the long uphill climb from the laundry. This climb ran close to the nurses' home and complaints from night staff who were woken up every time the loco passed were frequent. It was none of these factors which killed the line, however.

The resident doctors, who always seem to find some way of finding unusual enjoyment, had a fatal fascination for the railway. Sometimes they would spend all night playing with the loco and at the finish would derail all the wagons just for fun. In 1920 an in-experienced resident took over the controls for the first time and drove down the gradient at full speed. Only then did he realise that he did not know how to stop, and baled out just before the loco left the rails and plunged through the wall of the nurses' home. Never before had this sanctuary been breached and an enraged matron ensured that there was a vacancy on the medical staff next morning! The loco was taken back to the builders who could do nothing. Soon most of the rails were lifted and the space filled in with cement. The 135-foot stretch at the boiler house still remains, however, as does the centre block siding. In 1960, when the author was a resident in this famous institution, the route of the line remained obvious, and remarkably on the centre block siding remained one wagon! The line had been totally forgotten and the sub-basement now saw little use. The Infirmary Authorities allowed me access to all past records concerning the railway but shortly afterwards went to the trouble of scrapping the remaining wagon. The line may have been short and inconspicuous, but it was the first electrically powered line in Glasgow, and adds a new builder to the lists of those involved in Scotland's once famous locomotive construction industry.

**The Glasgow Royal Infirmary boiler house in 1937, below which the underground railway ran. Photo Andrew McDonald.**

Hartwood Hospital, the railway swung behind the hospital buildings from the right and terminated by the tall chimney in the centre.

# HARTWOOD HOSPITAL

*Also known as:*
   Lanark District Asylum
   Hartwood Asylum
   Hartwood Mental Hospital

In 1886 the Kirklands District Joint Lunacy Board (representing Lanarkshire, Govan and Glasgow) saw the need for more provision for their pauper lunatics. Over 600 acres of land were purchased from Lord Deas on his Hartwood Estate, set eighteen miles east of Glasgow. In 1888 the board was changed and the Lanark District Lunacy Board took over the management of the construction of the hospital. Building started in 1890 and over 75,000 tons of building materials were transported to the site; there was also a vast amount of earth moving, as two reservoirs had to be built holding 8,000 and 5,000 gallons of water. The Cleland and Midcalder line of the Caledonian Railway ran alongside the hospital site and was close to Hartwood Station. The station had opened in 1869 and was part of the main line between Glasgow and Edinburgh. The building contractors had constructed a railway line from the mainline, through a deep cutting to the rear of the hospital, to carry the tons of materials needed to build the hospital. Once construction was complete the railway was taken over by the hospital management and continued to run as a private railway. The hospital had its own locomotive, an 0-4-0 'Pug' saddle tank built in 1904, with the owner's name "Hartwood Asylum" prominently displayed and some hospital owned wagons. Some sources have identified an unusual covered open-

Hartwood had its own wagon. This has been described as a passenger carriage.

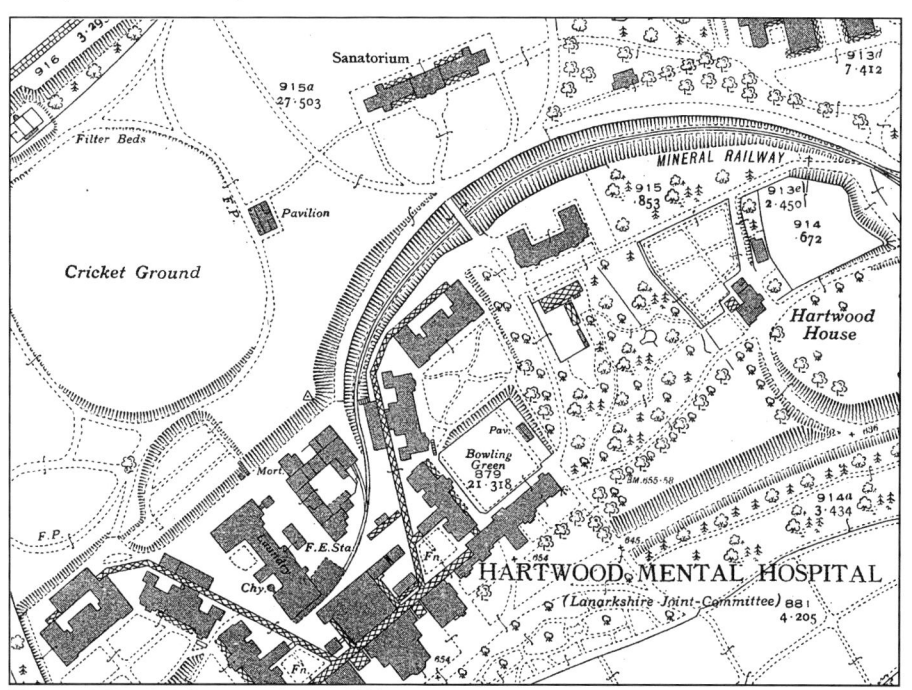

Hartwood Hospital Ordnance Survey 1939.

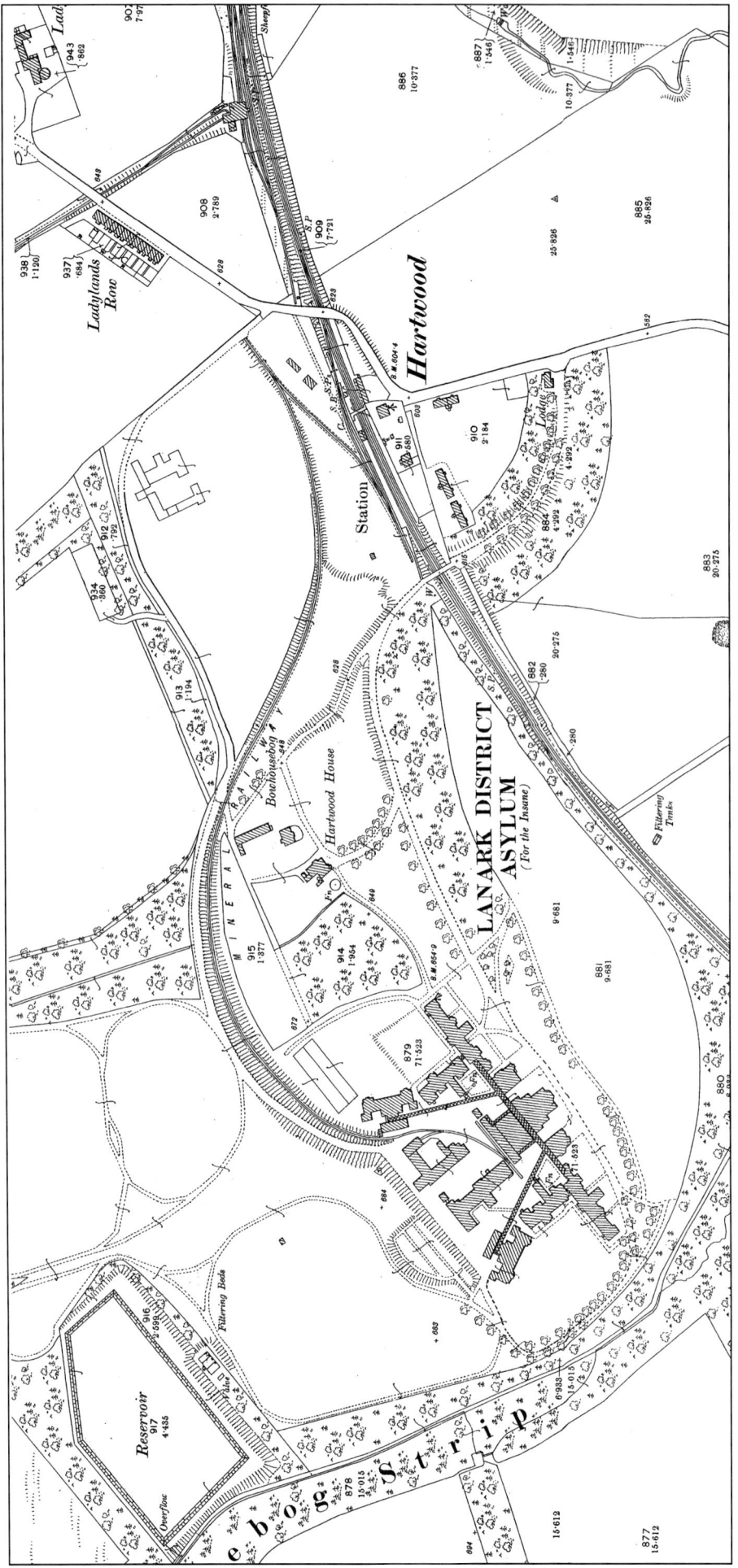

**Hartwood Hospital Railway Ordnance Survey 1898.**

sided wagon as a passenger vehicle. The 1898 map shows a siding running across the back of the main building, suggesting that passengers were carried on the line. At Hartwood station the hospital line ran along the island platform, again suggesting passenger use. By the 1939 map the siding along the back of the main building had been removed.

The new hospital opened in May 1895 with beds for 500 patients. The building cost £152,430 and a further £10,000 was spent on furnishings. The staff consisted of three doctors, six administrative staff, 25 male attendants, 17 female nurses, 12 servants and seven artisans and tradesmen. Hartwood grew rapidly and by 1901 it had beds for 730 patients, of whom 44 were private.

Like other similar hospitals the site had its own boiler house. At Hartwood there were some nine and a half miles of heating pipes. Electricity was also produced in its own generating plant. The reservoirs and the main line railway were protected with seven-foot high fences, to prevent patients getting access to them and doing themselves harm. In 1897 a further purchase was made of Home Farm, bringing the total size of the hospital to around 2,000 acres. The farm, as well as providing work for the patients, also gave a further reason for the private railway, as produce could be taken to Glasgow or Edinburgh markets, while bulk farm supplies would be brought in by train.

By 1913 the hospital had increased its capacity to nearly 1,000 patients and was at the time the largest asylum in Scotland. The sporting facilities included a bowling green, tennis court, croquet lawn, curling rink, cricket pitch, football pitch and a nine-hole golf course.

The generation plant was removed in 1932 when the power was purchased from the local supplier. As with so many private hospital railways, road transport overtook the railway for bringing in coal and it was no longer economic to keep it running. So the line closed in 1945.

A few of the old buildings of the original hospital survived to 2004 and though listed they were involved in a major fire in June, making the building unsafe. Hartwoodhill Hospital, built close by, still continues to serve as a hospital. However, the original Hartwood Hospital site has been offered for sale.

# LADYSBRIDGE HOSPITAL

*Also known as:*
**Banffshire County Lunatic Asylum**

I was told about this hospital following the publication of the first edition of the book. But it is difficult to determine the exact relationship between the hospital and Ladysbridge Station on the Banff, Portsoy and Strathisla Railway. The hospital and station were located just east of the village of Boyndie some three miles west of the coastal town of Banff. The first to arrive was the railway and the station. It was opened in 1859 to connect Grange (on the Aberdeen to Keith line) with the coast at Portsoy and Banff. There was a small community named after the crossing over the Burn of Boyndie, Lady's Bridge. The railway combined the name to give Ladysbridge Station its name.

The site was chosen to house the new Banffshire County Lunatic Asylum. Building was completed in 1865, some six years after the railway opened. It is probable that material for the buildings was transported by rail to the station, which was only a short distance from the hospital. There is no record of any contractor's railway, so the final distance would have been covered by road transport. The hospital had a Tudor style design, costing £12,000, with beds for 90 patients.

In keeping with the style of the period, the hospital gas works was sited some distance from the main hospital buildings, indeed the plant was closer to the houses on the edge of the town of Ladysbridge than to the hospital! The gas plant was alongside the road from the station to the town. Coal wagons would be delivered to the single siding of the station and then taken by road for the final short distance to the hospital gas plant. No records of the ending of the coal traffic have been found, but in

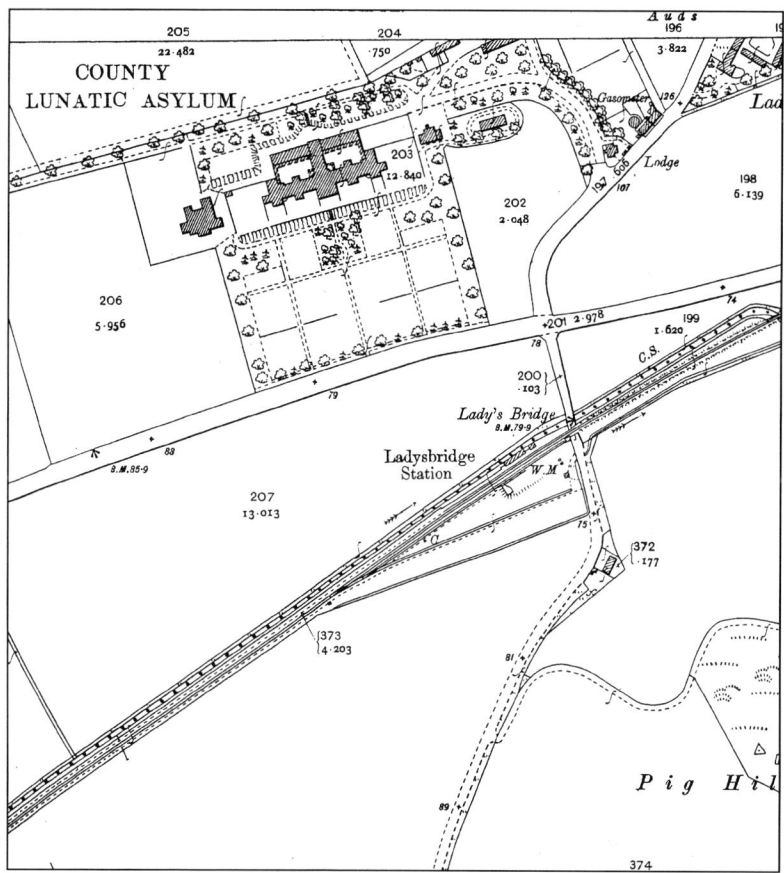

**Ladysbridge Hospital, Ordnance Survey 1904.**

common with other similar hospitals it is likely to have been in the 1950s or 60s. The railway closed to passengers in 1964 and finally closed to freight traffic in 1968.

Ladysbridge Hospital closed in 2001. On 6 October 2002 a special event, called "Celebration of the Life of Ladysbridge", was held in the main hall of the hospital building. With dancing to live music and a buffet, it was an opportunity for former patients and staff to reunite. This is the last recorded use of the hospital building.

# LENNOX CASTLE HOSPITAL

*Also known as:*
**Lennox Castle Certified Institution for Mental Defectives**

The story of Lennox Castle Hospital began in 1833 when John Lennox Kincaid-Lennox inherited the estate of the Lennox family in Woodhead, about nine miles north of Glasgow and beside the Campsie Fells. He petitioned the House of Lords to restore the family title of Earl of Lennox. His plans included building a castle that would be fitting for an Earl. The initial idea was to extend the Woodhead mansion. This proved impractical and it was decided to build a new castle, to be called Lennox Castle. Designed by David Hamilton, building commenced in 1837 and it was completed in 1841. The cost of the building depleted his funds so much that he had to abandon his petition for the Earldom.

In 1914 the Castle was requisitioned for use as a military hospital. To improve access to the hospital for wounded soldiers a siding was built to link the site with the Blane Valley branch of the North British Railway (NBR). The railway had been built in 1866 as the Blane Valley Railway, with Campsie Glen Station being built just north of the Lennox Estate. In 1881 the railway was absorbed into the North British Railway. After the war the castle was returned to the family.

The provision for the mentally handicapped in Glasgow had been met by opening Stoneyetts Hospital in 1913. However, it became seriously overcrowded and the Council had to seek more accommodation. Before anything could be done the First World War started and thoughts of new hospitals were put to one side. After the war the Council turned again to the need for more accommodation and after searching for suitable sites it

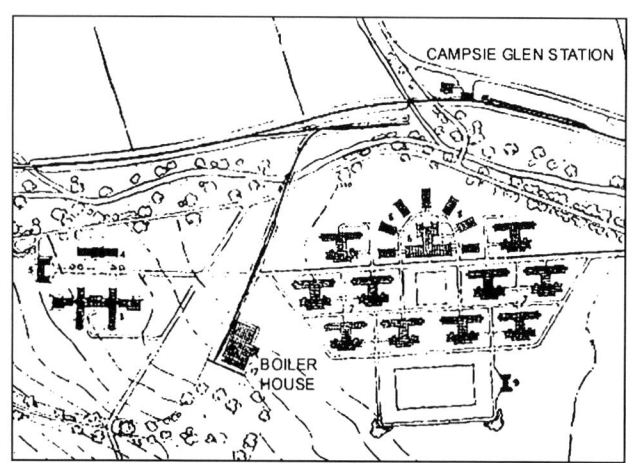

**Lennox Castle Hospital, detail of the railway from the 1936 book.**

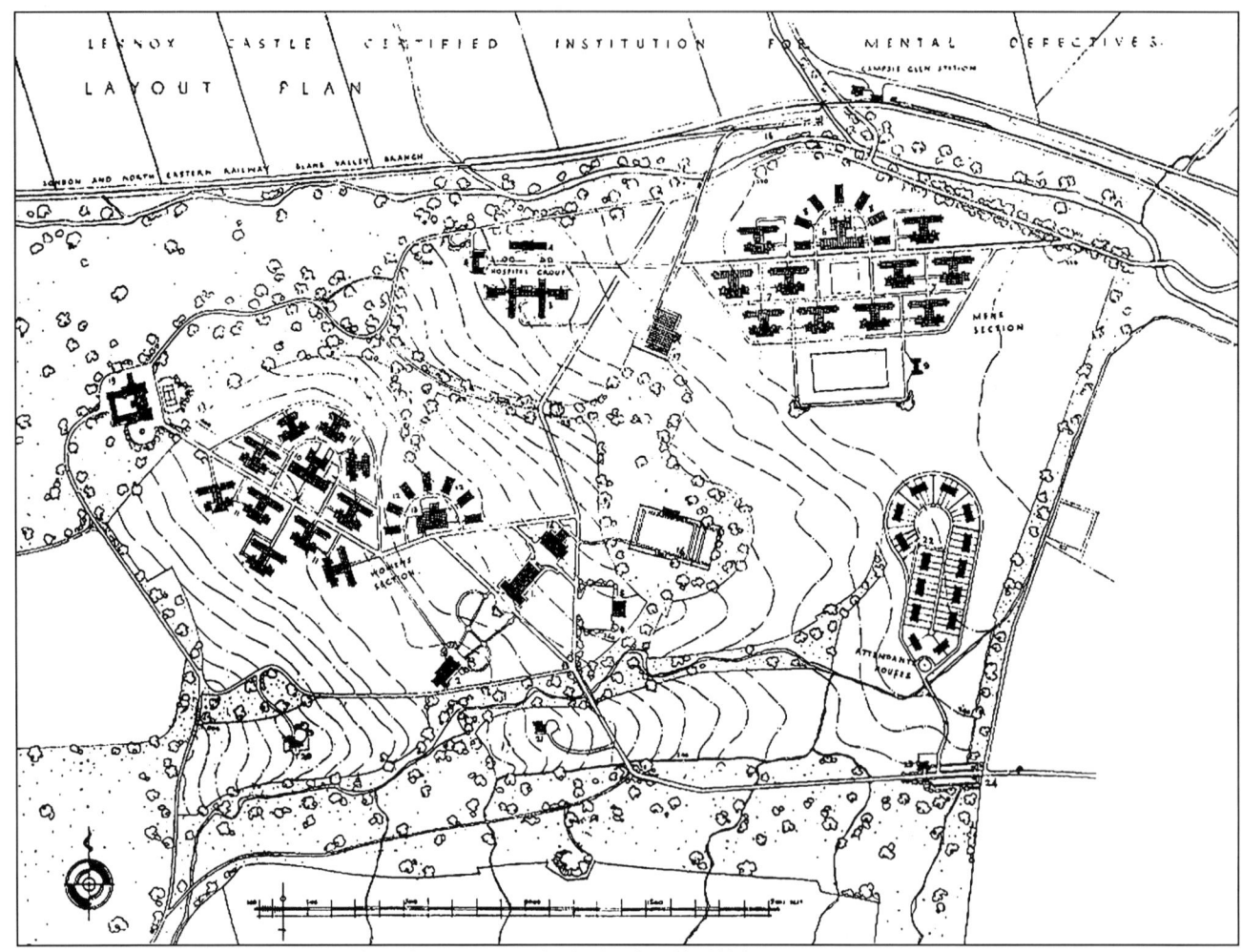

**Lennox Castle and the link to the LNER from the commemorative book printed in 1936.**

purchased the 122 acres, including the castle, of the Lennox estate in 1927 from William Lennox for the sum of £25,000. The intention from the start was to convert it to an institution for mentally handicapped patients, who previously had been accommodated in the same hospitals as psychiatric patients. The new institution required large buildings. Some three million bricks and 55,000 cubic feet of stone were used in the construction, delivered to the site by rail. During the construction the castle itself was used to accommodate female patients and the associated staff. The book printed in 1936 to commemorate the opening of the hospital "The Book of Lennox Castle" states that a private railway line was put in connecting the Blane Valley line of the London and North Eastern Railway with the power house. This infers that the private railway was not the same as the line laid in 1914 when the castle was used as a military hospital. Presumably the 1914 line was removed after the war.

The main hospital was formally opened in September 1936 with accommodation for 1,200 patients. The original castle building had been converted into accommodation for the nursing staff. Following the opening of the main hospital the railway was

**The official photograph of the staff at the opening of Hartwood hospital in 1895.**

**A poor photograph, but historic, as it shows the official opening of the hospital in 1936.**

used to transport goods, mainly coal to the boiler house. The line was about 800 yards long and had two passing loops for storing wagons, a weighbridge and associated office. It is not known whether the hospital had any privately owned wagons. It is also unlikely that any passengers were ever carried on the line, particularly as Campsie Glen Station was so close to the hospital grounds. In 1939 the hospital was requisitioned again by the War Office, under the Emergency Hospital provisions. The accommodation of the hospital was increased with the provision of temporary huts (that were still in use forty years later).

In 1941 a maternity unit was opened and expanded in 1948. This did cause an issue between the Mental Health Committee and the maternity services. The Committee complained that patients could not be allowed on ground parole because of the proximity of the maternity facilities. The main line railway north of the hospital was closed in 1959, leaving only the link with Glasgow, allowing coal trains to continue to supply the hospital via the hospital siding.

The maternity unit was closed in 1964, enabling the main hospital to take over the beds. It was this year, in September, that the siding was closed and the link to the railway was removed. The hospital itself was closed in June 2002. The original castle building has been listed, but has not been restored. The remainder of the site is destined for housing development.

**I have not been able to find any photographs of the railway. So here is the magnificent castle, used by the hospital as a nurses' home.**

# MURTHLY HOSPITAL

*Also known as:*
**Perth District Asylum**
**Murthly War Hospital**

In the 1800s the main psychiatric hospital for Perthshire was James Murray's Asylum, opened in 1827. Like other counties there was pressure on the facilities and the Perthshire Lunacy Board decided to commission a new hospital. The site chosen was beside the village of Murthly, some nine to ten miles north of Perth and beside the River Tay. The land purchased included an ancient stone circle, consisting of five stones in a circle about 30 feet in diameter.

The site was about ¼-mile north of Murthly Station (opened in 1856), providing a convenient means of transport for building materials and later passengers and coal for the hospital. It seems that the proximity of the station was a factor in the decision to purchase the land. The Lunacy Board had been in contact with the owners of the railway in 1861 regarding the construction of a siding to the proposed hospital. A siding is shown on the 1863 Ordnance Survey map, a year before the hospital opened. So it is likely that the siding was used during the construction of the buildings. This first siding is a single line from north west of Murthly Station to a small group of buildings including a gasometer and ending in a wagon turntable. These were the gas plant and were located suitably distant from the main hospital buildings. By 1901 two extra sidings had been laid from the wagon turntable, a short one alongside the gas plant and a second longer one to the main hospital buildings.

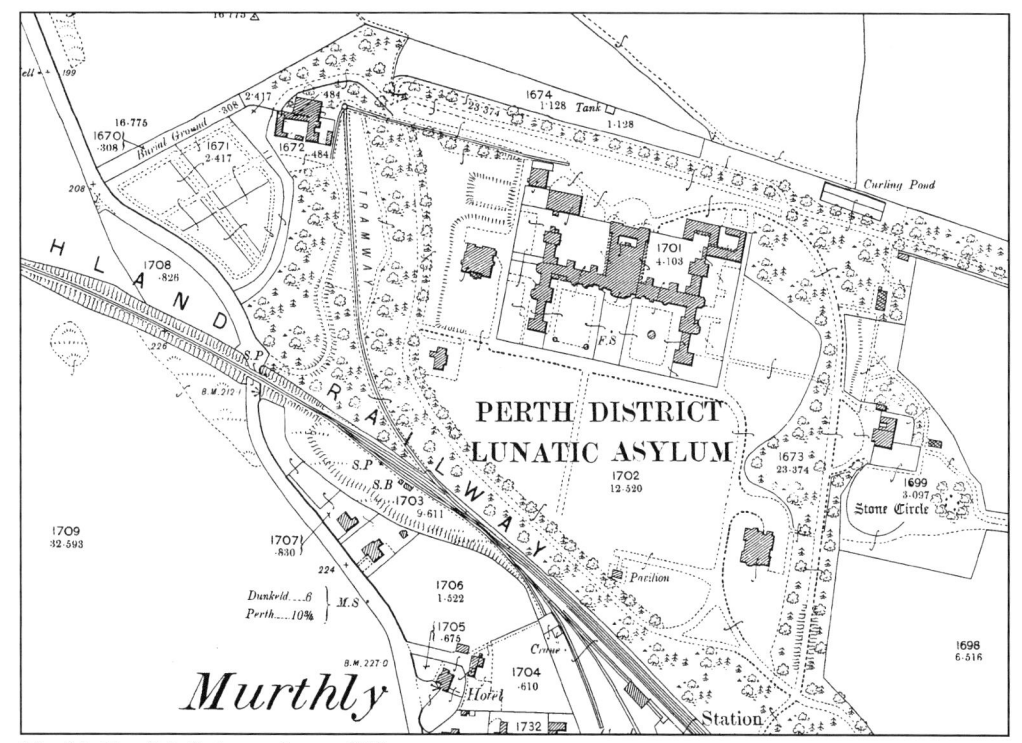

**Murthly Hospital, Ordnance Survey 1901.**

The hospital cost £30,000 initially and was extended in the 1890s at a cost of a further £10,000. It had accommodation for 260 patients.

The first Superintendent of the new hospital was William McIntosh. He had worked at James Murray's Asylum and was appointed to the new post at the age of 26. Although his training and work was in the field of medicine his obsession was marine biology. He eventually became Professor of Civil and Natural History at St Andrews and became one of the leading zoologists of his generation.

After the opening of the hospital the siding continued to be used. Like all other similar institutions the main commodity using the siding was coal. The hospital was as self sufficient as possible. It would produce its own town gas for heating and lighting. Later boilers and generators would have been installed for producing electricity. Both would have required large amounts of coal. The siding was on a falling gradient towards the gas plant. Full coal wagons would arrive at Murthly on a goods train. They would be shunted just inside the siding gate on hospital grounds and the brakes pinned down. Then hospital staff would take them to the gas plant. It is likely that they were allowed to roll by gravity down to the plant for unloading. Once empty the wagons would probably have been hauled back to the siding gate by a horse.

The hospital did not own either a locomotive nor rolling stock and there is no record of any passengers ever having been carried on the line. Indeed it was about as far to the hospital from the gas plant as it was from Murthly Station. So all staff and visitors would disembark at the main line station and walk the few hundred yards to the hospital.

It is probable that the line fell out of use in the late 1950s or early 1960s when hospital boilers were converted to oil burning. As there was no rolling stock, there is no record of when the last wagon used the siding. The rails remained in place and were reported as having no traffic but still usable in 1965. The railway line is still in use and provides rail access to Inverness, Perth, Glasgow and Edinburgh. However, Murthly station itself closed.

Murthly Hospital closed in 1984. It and the land was sold in 1987/88 for private housing development. The estate is now called Druids Park. The stone circle is on private land (the garden of Druids Park House), while the remaining land has become executive style housing.

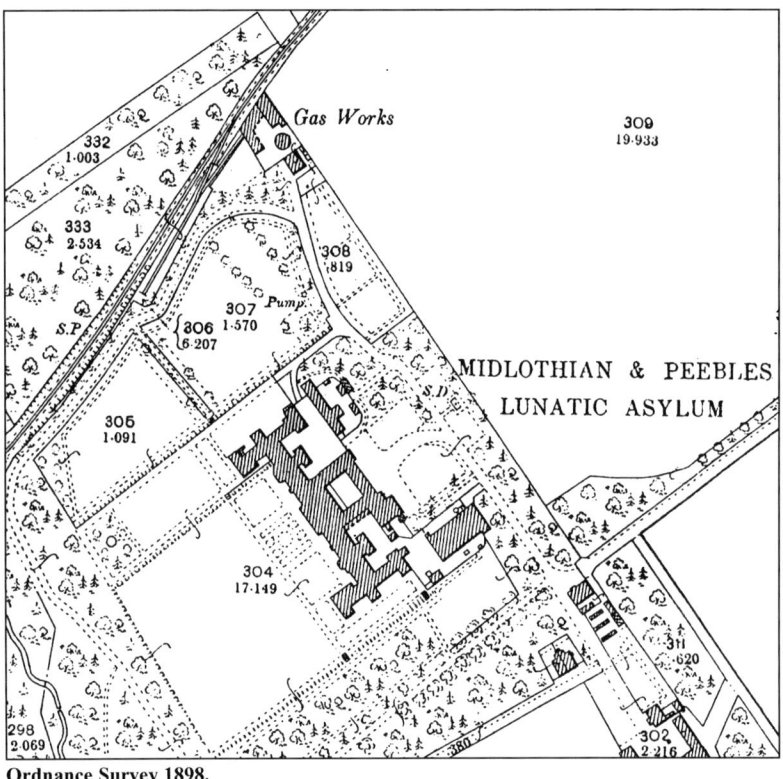

---

**Ordnance Survey 1898.**

**Site of the Rosslynlee Hospital Halt platform. The hospital buildings are behind the trees. There are no traces of the wooden platform, and the site is covered in trees and shrubs**

# ROSSLYNLEE HOSPITAL

*Also known as:*
**Counties Lunatic Asylum**
**Midlothian and Peebles Lunatic Asylum**
**Midlothian and Peebles District Asylum**

Rosslynlee Hospital opened in 1874. It was built right next to the Peebles Railway (opened in 1855 and absorbed by the North British Railway in 1876). During the building of the hospital a siding was built in the hospital grounds, connecting with the NBR line. It is likely that the building materials for the hospital were brought by rail and unloaded using the siding. When the hospital was completed in 1874 the siding was used to convey coal to supply the hospital gas works.

The initial name for the hospital was the Counties Lunatic Asylum (Midlothian and Peebles). This later became the Midlothian and Peebles Lunatic Asylum, then the Midlothian and Peebles District Asylum, finally becoming Rosslynlee Hospital, named after the nearby town and railway station.

In 1958 a new Halt platform was built beside the hospital and called Rosslynlee Hospital Halt. The wooden platform was built on the land that had been used for the siding. However, the life of the station was destined to be very short as the railway closed to passengers in 1962, and then it completely closed in 1967. The site of the platform is just about recognisable for those knowing what to look for, but the wooden platform has completely disappeared.

In 1998 it was recognised that the hospital buildings were no longer suitable and plans were drawn up for a new hospital. However, difficulties over planning approval have meant that the new building has been delayed. Following a public enquiry planning permission was given for a new Midlothian Community Hospital in Bonnyrigg.

# ROYAL SCOTTISH NATIONAL HOSPITAL

*Also known as:*
**Scottish Institution for the Education of Imbecile Children**
**Scottish National Institution for the Education of Imbecile Children**
**Scottish National Hospital**

In the early Victorian period facilities for mentally handicapped children were scarce and local authorities had neither the obligation or will to make any provisions. However public opinion was changing, and led by individuals and charitable bodies schools were being set up in various parts of Europe. The first specialist school in Scotland was established in 1855 near Dundee with another in Edinburgh following quickly. In 1859 the Society for Education of Imbecile Youth in Scotland was founded in 1859 with the aim of providing a model institution in the Edinburgh area for children aged between six and twelve years. Fund raising was very slow until the idea of suggesting a penny subscription to raise many gifts of a small amount. This took off and £1,500 was raised. This allowed the Society to expand its fund-raising and considerable sums were raised. It had many eminent patrons, including Queen Victoria.

The very Victorian exterior of the main hospital building.

Steps were started to build the model institution. Unfortunately opposition in Edinburgh forced the society to look outside the city. In 1861 they selected a five-acre site just north of the small village of Larbert and purchased it. The site was particularly appropriate because it was beside a railway. The Scottish Central railway had built the line in 1848 and it had connections to every part of Scotland. The Society recognised that it could be used to bring building materials to the site and once the institution was built to provide an easy way for patients, staff and visitors to get to the site.

The institution was built over a number of years. The first building opened in 1863 at a cost of £13,000 and room for thirty children, though when it opened there were only nine. New buildings were added as funds became available. Indeed buildings were often completed but had to wait until sufficient money was raised to buy furniture. As mentioned before building materials were brought to the site by rail. The railway line by the site had a siding

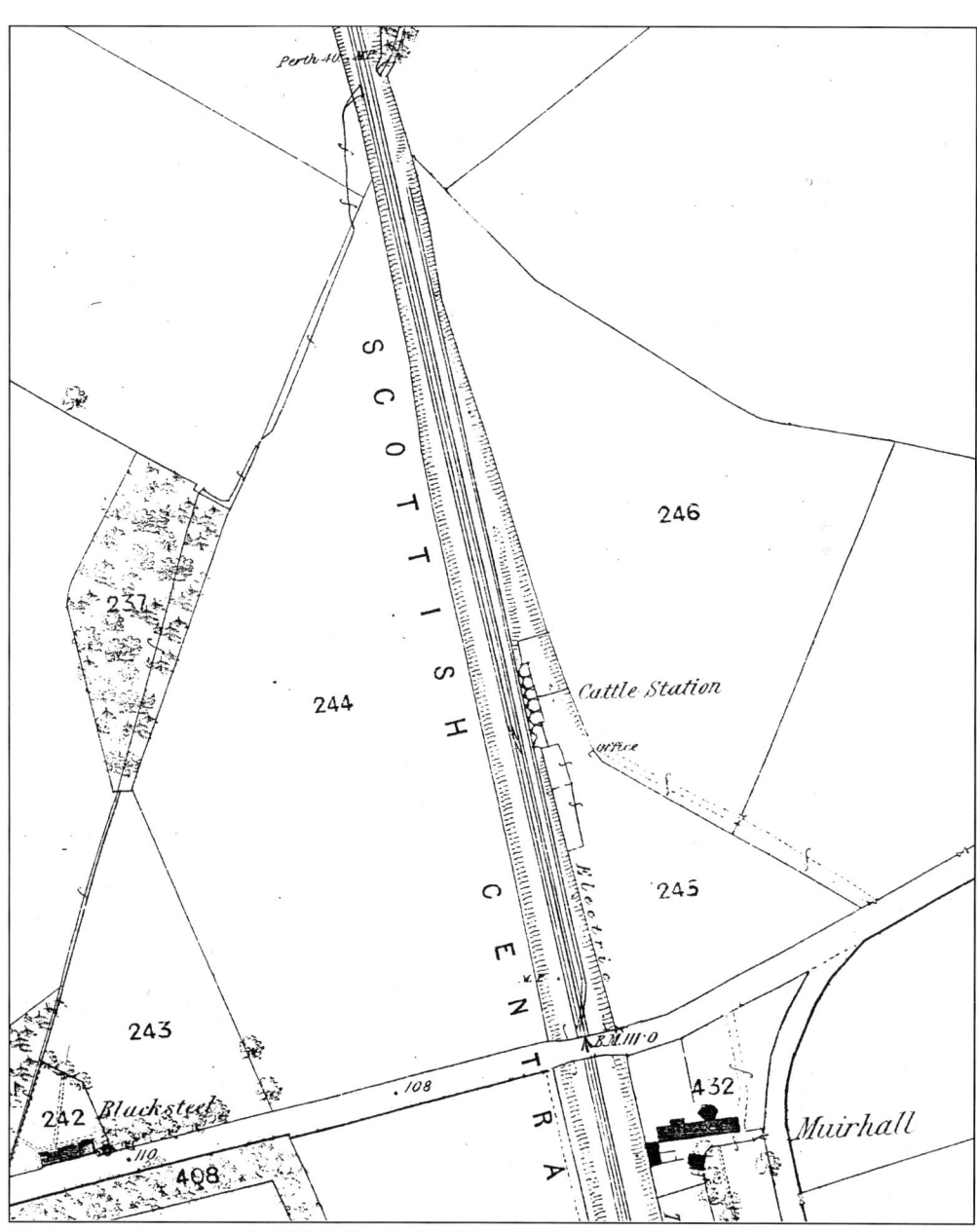

The Ordnance Survey map for 1860, before the hospital was built, showing the cattle siding.

71

already established, with a cattle dock. It is highly likely that this siding, although it was on the opposite side of the main line from the hospital, was used to deliver the vast quantities of materials needed by the hospital.

From the start the demand for places exceeded the availability. So a programme of expansion was started. By 1870 there were 75 children in the hospital and 350 in 1907. This expansion continued through to the First World War, when the lack of skilled craftsmen meant that the limited building work was very delayed. In 1916 King George V granted the honour of adding 'Royal' to the name.

In the 1930s the Society purchased the Lambert House and adjoining estate. A new community unit was built for adults with learning difficulties. It was known as the 'Colony' and had a large farm, gardens and workshops where people could work to provide food and clothing for the Institution.

Ordnance Survey maps of the area show that the cattle siding continued to exist in the same form after the opening of the hospital. While it cannot be said precisely, it is likely that there were no special facilities built by the railway to serve the hospital. Although the opportunity was there, no rail connection was ever made into the hospital grounds. It would seem that visitors, staff and patients used Larbert Station, as it was a convenient three quarters of a mile from the hospital.

Like other such hospitals the NHS took both sites over in 1948. In the 1980s came a change of policy and the removal of large institutions. Instead they were replaced with community care. The Royal Scottish National Hospital was gradually run down until it closed in 2003. The name continues in a smaller unit within Larbert. However the original sites are being developed for housing and commercial use. Some of the buildings may be preserved as a reminder of the work that the hospital did.

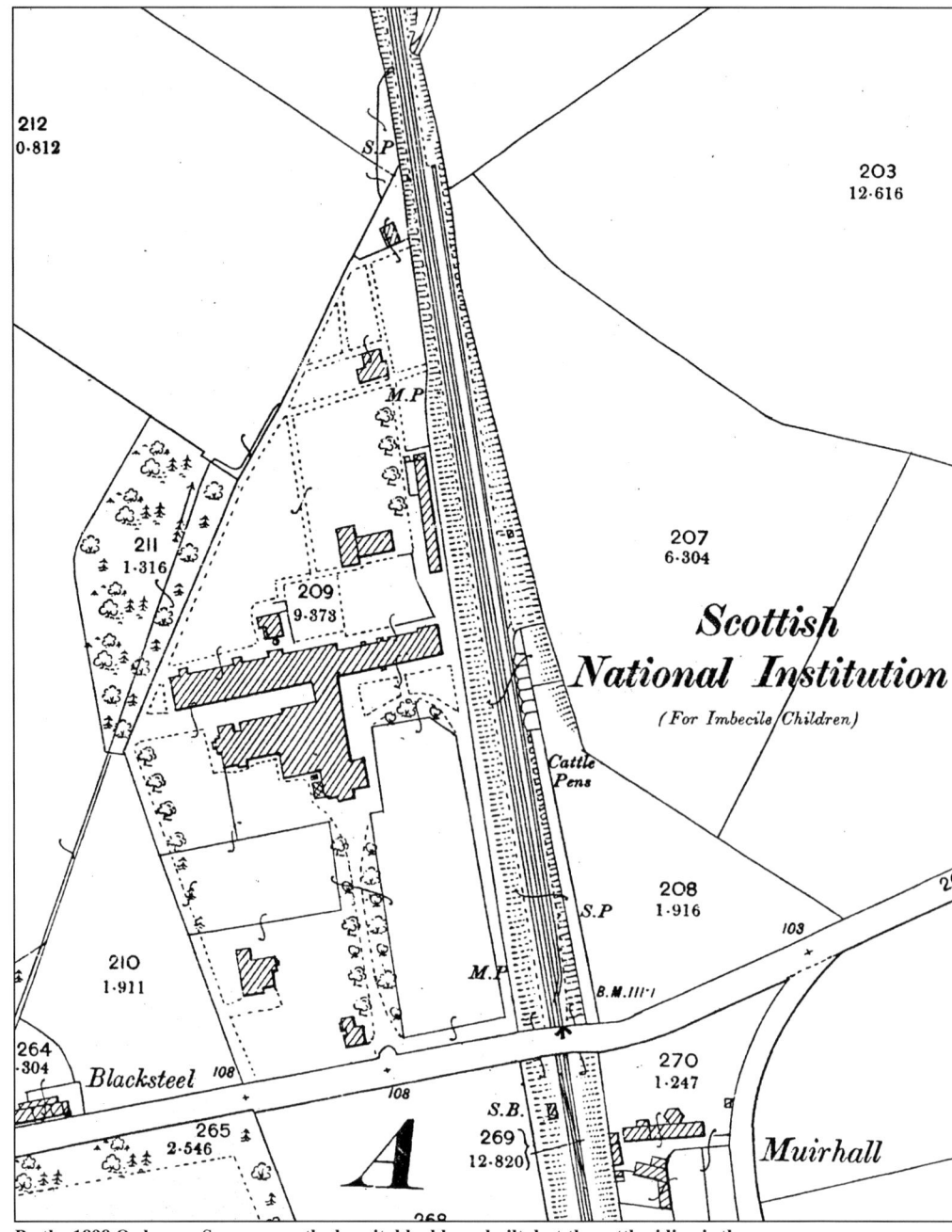

**By the 1898 Ordnance Survey map the hospital had been built, but the cattle siding is the same.**

# WELSH HOSPITAL RAILWAY

## PRINCE OF WALES HOSPITAL

The War Office identified a need for facilities to treat wounded soldiers who had lost limbs during the First World War. A site was selected at Rhydlafar Farm, just north of Cardiff and the military hospital was built. The name of the hospital was agreed by the then Prince of Wales, later Edward VIII and then Duke of Windsor, who formally opened the hospital on 20 February 1918. The event was filmed by the Stoll Film Company. This shows the arrival of the Prince of Wales at the hospital and footage of the patients. Groups of patients with artificial limbs were photographed going around a "Miniature Wild Wales", a circular track made to represent the rougher terrain of rural Wales. The aim was to rehabilitate the men so they could return to civilian life. The film starkly shows the devastation of the injuries afflicting the patients.

The hospital made use of an existing siding at Crofft-y-Genau. Although the Brecon and Merthyr Railway actually passed along the eastern boundary of the hospital grounds, the Crofft-y-Genau siding on the Taff Vale Railway was preferred. This siding was to the south of the hospital, was readily available and it was alongside a road leading to the hospital grounds. The siding was well used, supplying the needs of the hospital.

In the Second World War the hospital was managed by the American Army and again the siding saw extensive use, taking supplies to the hospital. It is not known if Ambulance Trains used the siding. After the end of the war it was decided that the hospital should be taken over by the NHS and be converted into an orthopaedic hospital. At the time this was one of the largest and most expensive conversions to take place in the NHS. It continued to serve the public as an orthopaedic hospital, though

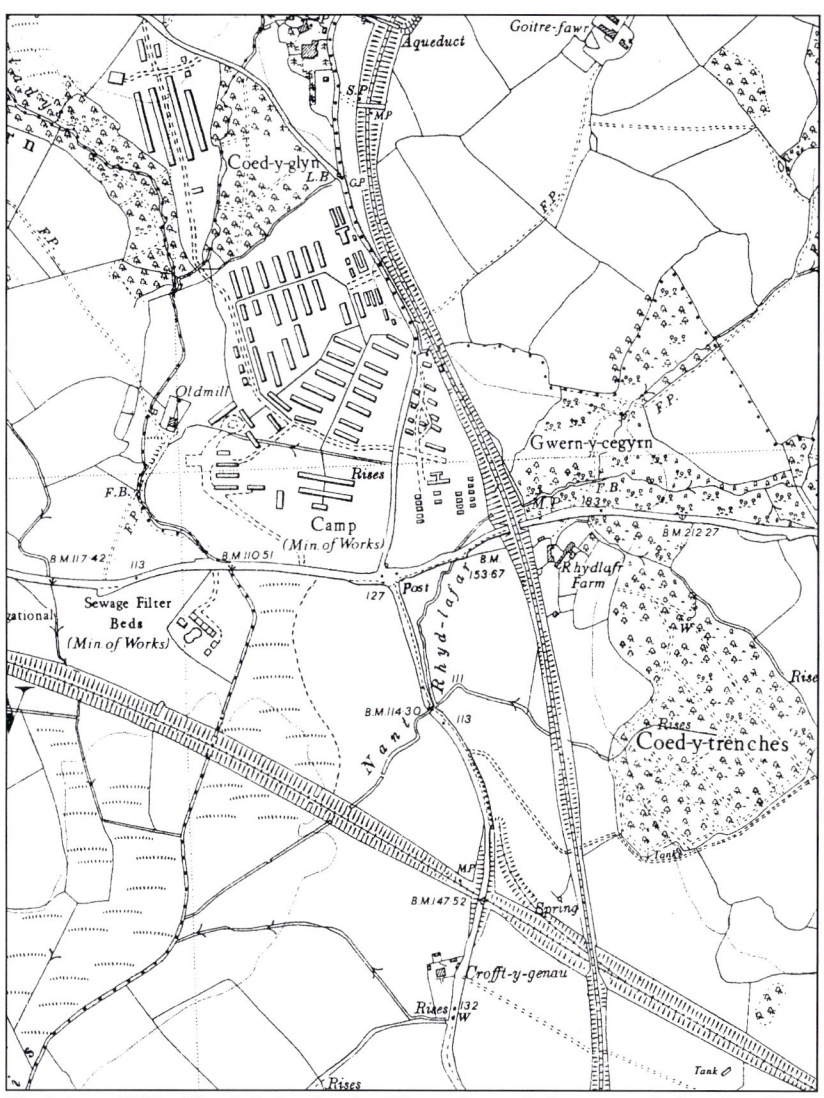

**The Prince of Wales Hospital, showing the siding to the south that was used when the military occupied the hospital. Ordnance Survey 1948.**

the railway siding was not used for hospital purposes.

With the re-organisations in the NHS at the end of the 20th century, it was considered that there was no further need for the hospital. The Bro Taff Health Authority sold the site for £10 million in November 2000. The site will be used for residential development.

# ACKNOWLEDGEMENTS AND SOURCES

This book would not have been possible without the wonderful public libraries that our country is blessed with. In many instances I was able to visit the libraries and record offices concerned and in every instance my queries were answered quickly, efficiently and most of all cheerfully. For libraries beyond my travelling limits I wrote explaining my queries. Again the response was always extremely helpful and often took me in further directions I had not expected. To all those librarians and archivists I would like to pass my sincere gratitude.

The major source of information has come from the writings of previous researchers and historians. The major works I used are listed below. I also came across unpublished papers held in local libraries and written by those who worked in the hospitals. These first-hand accounts gave a real feeling for what life was like to be part of the hospital community. There is a greater emphasis these days on recording local history from local people and this is an enormous resource for future generations.

Following publication of the first edition a number of people have been in touch with valuable information enabling this second and enlarged edition to be produced. I would particularly like to thank Alan Brotchie, Alan Kirkman, Peter Michie and other members of the North West Group of the Industrial Locomotive Society, Roger Monk, John Payne and Derek Persson for their help.

## GENERAL

*A Guide to Private Siding Problems* by William Oldham (Industrial Transport Publications Ltd. 1930)
*Private and Untimetabled Railway Stations Halts and Stopping Places* by Godfrey Croughton, R.W. Kidner and Alan Young (Oakwood Press 1982)
*Ordnance Survey maps*, six inches to the mile and three inches to the mile, between 1890 and 1948.

## ENGLISH HOSPITAL TRAMWAYS AND RAILWAYS

**Addenbrookes Hospital**
*Report to Environment Scrutiny Committee 27/04/2004* by Head of Policy and Projects, Cambridge City Council
*Waterbeach Briefing* by RWL Estates Ltd., September 2002

**Cumberland and Westmorland Convalescent Institution**
*Solway Steam* by Stephen White (Carel Press 1984)
*The Silloth Branch* by Alan Earnshaw (Back Track July-August 1990 and September-October 1990)

**Epsom Hospitals**
*Epsom's Hospital Railway* by R.I. Essen (Author 1991)
*A Guide to the Industrial History of Epsom and Ewell* by Peter Wakefield (Surrey Industrial History Group 1997)
*Racing to Residential: the Wimbledon and Epsom Line* by Alan A. Jackson (Railway World July 1980)
*The Horton Light Railway* by Alan A. Jackson (Railway Magazine October 1981)
*Industrial Locomotives of South Eastern England.* Edited by Eric S. Tonks (Birmingham Locomotive Club, Industrial Locomotive Information Section 1958)

**Haslar Royal Navy Hospital**
*Gosport and Horndean Tramways* by Martin Petch (Middleton Press June 1997)

*The Tramways of the South Coast* by J.C. Gillham and R.J.S. Wiseman (Light Rail Transit Association 2004)

**Hellingly Hospital**
*The Hellingly Hospital Railway* by H.R. Stones (The Railway Magazine December 1957)
*The Railways of Southern England* by Edwin Course (B.T. Batsford Ltd 1976)
*The Hellingly Hospital Railway* (Bluebell News Spring 1978)
*The Hellingly Hospital Railway* by Peter A. Harding (Author 1989)
*The Tramways of the South Coast* by J.C. Gillham and R.J.S. Wiseman (Light Rail Transit Association 2004)

**High Royds Hospital**
*The Railways of Wharfedale* by Peter E. Baughan (David & Charles 1969)
*Menston Hospital's Railway 1888-1951* by F.E. Rogers (Keighley Gazette 19th September 1988)
*The Otley and Ilkley Joint Railway* by F.W. Smith and Martin Bairstow (Martin Bairstow 1992)
*Industrial Locomotives of West Yorkshire* by I.R. Bandall (Industrial Railway Society 2004)

**Joyce Green Hospital**
*London's Last Horse Tramway* by J.H. Price (Journal of Transport History, May 1962)
*The Tramways of Woolwich and South East London* by South Eastern (Light Rail Transit Association and Tramway and Light Railway Society 1963)
*North Kent Tramways* by Robert J. Harley (Middleton Press December 1994)
*Joyce Green and the River Hospitals* by Francine Payne (DWS Print Services Ltd 2001)

**Knowle Hospital**
*The Knowle Experience* by various authors (privately published)
*History of Knowle Hospital 1852-1884* by R. Bursell (Author 1976)
*The Railways of Southern England: Independent Lines* by E. Course (Batsford, 1976)

**Lord Mayor Treloar's Hospital**
*The Railways of Southern England* by Edwin Course (B.T. Batsford Ltd 1976)
*The Basingstoke and Alton Light Railway* by Edward Griffith (Kingfisher Railway Productions 1982)
*The Basingstoke and Alton Light Railway* by Martin Dean, Kevin Robertson & Roger Simmonds (Crusader Press 1998)
*Southern Railway Branch Line Trains* by R.W. Kidner (Oakwood Press 1984)

**Netley Military Hospital**
*The Railways of Southern England* by Edwin Course (B.T. Batsford Ltd 1976)
*Netley Hospital and Its Railways* by J.R. Fairman (Kingfisher Railway Productions 1984)
*The Southampton and Netley Railway* by Edwin Course (City of Southampton)
*Southern Railway Branch Line Trains* by R.W. Kidner (Oakwood Press 1984)

**Park Prewett Hospital**
*The Park Prewett Hospital Railway, Basingstoke* by Roger Simmonds

*Park Prewett Hospital Railway* by John Fairman (Railway Observer March 1970)
*The Railways of Southern England* by Edwin Course (B.T. Batsford Ltd 1976)
*Basingstoke, 150 Years of Railway Progress* by J.R. Fairman (1987)

**Queen Mary's Hospital For Children**
*Queen Mary's Hospital For Children* by Ernest Earl (Able Publishing Services 1996)
*A Vision of Healing Queen Mary's Hospital for Children Volume 2* by Ernest Earl (Able Publishing Services 2001)
*Corridor Train* by Dudley Alexander (published by the author 1967)

**St Edwards Hospital**
*North Staffordshire County Mental Hospital Railway* (Stevenson Locomotive Society Magazine June 1957)
*A History of St Edward's Hospital* by Max Chadwick and David Pearson (Churnet Valley Books 1993)
*The Tramway of St Edward's Hospital Cheddleton* by David Voice (Tramway Review Spring 1996)
*Industrial Locomotives of North Staffordshire* by Alan C. Baker (Industrial Railway Society 1997)
*The St Edward's (Cheddleton) Hospital Railway* by J. Atyeo (Railway Bylines July 1999)

**Scalebor Park Hospital**
*Industrial Locomotives of West Yorkshire* by I.R. Bandall (Industrial Railway Society 2004)

**Three Counties Hospital**
*A Place in the Country, Three Counties Asylum 1860-1998* by Judith Pettigrew, Rory W. Reynolds and Sandra Rouse (South Bedfordshire Community Health Care Trust 1998)
*Railways in Bedfordshire* by Sandy Chrystal (Reflections of a Bygone Age 2000)
*Hitchin to Peterborough* by Vic Mitchell and Allan Mott (Middleton Press May 2003)
*Industrial Locomotives of Buckinghamshire, Bedfordshire & Northamptonshire* by Robin Waywell (Industrial Railway Society 2001)

**Whittingham Hospital**
*The Whittingham Railway* by H. C. Casserley (The Railway Magazine May 1957)
*Affray at Whittingham* by Norman Jones (The Railway Magazine May 1958)
*Grimsargh Junction, Change Here for Whittingham* by David Hindle (Steam Days May 2004)
*Grimsargh, The Story of a Lancashire Village* by David Hindle (Carnegie Publishing 2002)

# WAR-TIME TEMPORARY MILITARY HOSPITALS IN ENGLAND

**General**
*War on the Line* by Bernard Darwin (Southern Railway Company 1946)
*The South-Eastern & Chatham Railway in the 1914-18 War* by David Gould (Oakwood Press 1981)

**Bewdley US Military Hospital**
*The US Army at Camp Bewdley and Locations in the Wyre Forest Area 1943-1945* by Adrian and Neil Turley (Authors February 2000)

**Bulford Camp Military Hospital**
*Plain Soldiering* by Noel David Glaves James (The Hobnob Press 1987)
*Southern Railway Branch Line Trains* by R.W. Kidner (Oakwood Press 1984)
*Industrial Locomotives of Central Southern England* by Roger Hateley (Industrial Railway Society undated)

**Codford Camp Military Hospital**
*Plain Soldiering* by Noel David Glaves James (The Hobnob Press 1987)
*Industrial Locomotives of Central Southern England* by Roger Hateley (Industrial Railway Society undated)

**Fargo Military Hospital**
*Plain Soldiering* by Noel David Glaves James (The Hobnob Press 1987)
*Southern Railway Branch Line Trains* by R.W. Kidner (Oakwood Press 1984)
*Industrial Locomotives of Central Southern England* by Roger Hateley (Industrial Railway Society undated)

**Fovant Military Hospital**
*Plain Soldiering* by Noel David Glaves James (The Hobnob Press 1987)
*Southern Railway Branch Line Trains* by R.W. Kidner (Oakwood Press 1984)
*Industrial Locomotives of Central Southern England* by Roger Hateley (Industrial Railway Society undated)

**Ingress Abbey Military Hospital**
The South-Eastern & Chatham Railway in the 1914-18 War by David Gould (Oakwood Press 1981)

**Morley US Military Hospital**
*Wymondham College The First Fifty Years* by Roger Garrard & Michael Brand (Wymondham College Association 2001)

**Sutton Veny Military Hospital**
*Plain Soldiering* by Noel David Glaves James (The Hobnob Press 1987)

**Tidworth Camp Military Hospital**
*Plain Soldiering* by Noel David Glaves James (The Hobnob Press 1987)
*100 years of a Cotswold Railway Line* by Paul Strong (Back Track November-December 1992 and January-February 1993)
*Tidworth Military Railways* by C. Barber (The Bullet, The Journal of the Royal Corps of Transport Railway Society)

# SCOTTISH HOSPITAL TRAMWAYS AND RAILWAYS

**Bangour Hospital**
*Wee Bangour Express* by Peter B. Russell (Railway Magazine September 1981)

**Glasgow Royal Infiirmary**
*The Glasgow Royal Infirmary Railway, Glasgow's First Electrically Operated "Underground" Railway* by Dr I.D.O. Frew (Scottish Transport June 1972)

**Hartwood Hospital**
*Hartwood Hospital A Hundred Years 1895-1995* by Shotts Local History Group (Shotts Local History Group 1996)
*Industrial Locomotives of Scotland.* Edited by Alan Bridges (Industrial Railway Society 1976)

**Lennox Castle Hospital**
*The Book of Lennox Castle, Lennox Castle Mental Defectives Institution* by A.L. Richie (City and Counties Publishing Co. Ltd. 1936)

**Murthly Hospital**
*The Murthly Asylum Branch* (Highland Railway Journal, Nos 24 & 25, 1993)

**Royal Scottish National Hospital**
*The Royal Scottish National Hospital 140 Years* by Guthrie Hutton (Forth Valley Primary Care NHS Trust 2000)

# ADAM GORDON

**The Life of Isambard Kingdom Brunel**
  by his son, reprint of the 1870 edition, s/b, 604pp, £20
**The Cable System of Tramway Traction**
  reprint of 1896 publication, 56pp, s/b, £10
**The Definitive Guide to Trams (including Funiculars) in the British Isles**
  3rd edition; D. Voice, s/b, A5, 248pp, £20
**Double-Deck Trams of the World, Beyond the British Isles**
  B. Patton, A4 s/b, 180pp, £18
**Double-Deck Trolleybuses of the World, Beyond the British Isles**
  B. Patton, A4, s/b, 96pp, £16
**The Douglas Horse Tramway**
  K. Pearson, softback, 96 pp, £14.50
**Edinburgh Street Tramways Co Rules & Regulations**
  reprint of 1883 publication, s/b, 56 pp, £8
**Edinburgh's Transport, vol. 2**
  1919-1975, D. Hunter, 192pp, s/b, £20
**The Feltham Car of the Metropolitan Electric and London United Tramways**
  reprint of 1931 publication, s/b, 18pp, £5
**Glasgow Subway Album**
  G. Watson, A4 s/b, all colour, 64pp, £10
**How to Go Tram and Tramway Modelling**
  third edition, D. Voice, B4, 152pp, completely rewritten, s/b, £20
**London Transport Bus Routes, Central Area No.2 1943**
  reprint, £5
**Modern Tramway, reprint of volumes 1 & 2, 1938-1939**
  c.A4 cloth hardback, £38
**My 50 Years in Transport**
  A.G. Grundy, 54 pp, s/b, 1997, £10
**Omnibuses & Cabs, Their Origin and History**
  H.C. Moore, h/b reprint with d/w, 282pp, £25
**The Overhaul of Tramcars**
  reprint of LT publication of 1935, 26pp, s/b, £6
**Next Stop Seaton! – Golden Jubilee history of Modern Electric Tramways Ltd**
  David Jay & David Voice, B5 softback, 136pp, covers coloured on both sides, £17
**Source Book of Literature relating to Tramways in the East Midlands**
  36pp, £4
**Source Book of Literature relating to Tramways in South-West England**
  36pp, £4
**Source Book of Literature relating to Tramways in Merseyside & Cheshire**
  36pp, £4
**Source Book of Literature relating to Tramways in East Anglia**
  s/b, 28pp, £4
**Source Book of Literature relating to Tramways in the North East of England**
  28pp, £4

# PUBLICATIONS

**Source Book of Literature relating to Tramways in N. Lancashire & Cumbria**
39pp, s/b, £4

**Source Book of Literature relating to Tramways in South Central England**
26pp, £4

**Source Book of Literature relating to Tramways in Scotland**
48pp, £5

**Source Book of Literature relating to Welsh Tramways**
28pp, £4

**Source Book of Literature relating to Yorkshire Tramways**
52pp, £5.50

**The History of the Steam Tram**
H. Whitcombe, h/b, over 60pp, £12

**A History of the British Steam Tram**
volume 1, David Gladwin, case bound, coloured covers, 176pp, 312 x 237mm, profusely illustrated, £40

**Street Railways, their construction, operation and maintenance**
by C.B. Fairchild, reprint of 1892 publication, 496pp, hardback, profusely illustrated, £40

**Toy and Model Trams of the World – Volume 1: Toys, die casts and souvenirs**
Gottfried Kuře and David Voice, A4 s/b, all colour, 128pp, £25

**Toy and Model Trams of the World – Volume 2: Plastic, white metal and brass models and kits**
Gottfried Kuře and David Voice, A4 s/b all colour, 188pp, £30

**George Francis Train's Banquet**
report of 1860 on the opening of the Birkenhead tramway, reprint, s/b, 118pp, £10

**My Life in Many States and in Foreign Lands**
G.F. Train, reprint of his autobiography, over 350pp, s/b, £12

**Trams, Trolleybuses and Buses and the Law before De-regulation**
M. Yelton, B4, s/b, 108pp, £15

**Tramway Review, reprint of issues 1-16, 1950-1954**
A5 cloth hardback, £23

**Tramways and Electric Railways in the Nineteenth Century**
reprint of Electric Railway Number of Cassier's Magazine, 1899, cloth h/b, over 250pp, £23

**The Twilight Years of the trams in Aberdeen & Dundee**
all colour, A4 s/b, introduction and captions by A. Brotchie, 120pp, £25

**The Twilight Years of the Edinburgh Tram**
112pp, A4 s/b, incs 152 coloured pics, £25

**The Twilight Years of the Glasgow Tram**
over 250 coloured views, A4, s/b, 144 pp, £25

**The Wantage Tramway**
S.H. Pearce Higgins, with Introduction by John Betjeman, h/b reprint with d/w, over 158pp, £28

**The Wearing of the Green**
being reminiscences of the Glasgow trams, W. Tollan, s/b, 96pp, £12

# NON TRANSPORT PUBLICATIONS

**From Death Into Life**
W. Haslam, 250pp, s/b, £8. Autobiography of a clergyman converted by, or at least during, his own sermon!

**The Chateau Story**
Elizabeth Varley, 64pp, s/b, £10. An animal "fairy-tale" set in France in the reign of a King Louis, described as "a children's story for grown-ups, or a grown-up's story for children" – so ideal for any age!

## TERMS

**RETAIL UK-** for post and packing please add 10% of the value of the order up to £4.90 maximum, apart from the Brunel biography and Street Railways, which because of their weight, please add £3, and £5 respectively. Orders £50 and over post and packing free. I regret that I am not yet equipped to deal with credit/debit cards.

**RETAIL OVERSEAS** – postage will be charged at printed paper rate via surface mail, unless otherwise requested. Payment please by sterling cash or cheque, UK sterling postage stamps, or direct bank to bank by arrangement.

**SOCIETIES, CHARITIES,** etc. relating to tramways, buses and railways – a special 50% discount for any quantity of purchases is given **provided my postal charges are paid**.

**WHOLESALE (TRADE) DISCOUNTS FOR MULTIPLE COPIES OF THE SAME TITLE, UK** post free:
1-15 copies – 35%; 16-30 copies – 40%; 31-45 copies – 45%; 46 & over – 50%

---

Apart from being a publisher of tramway titles I buy and sell secondhand literature. I issue lists 3 or 4 times a year which contain a variety of books, periodicals, timetables, postcards, tickets and "special/unusual material"; postage is charged at cost and there is no charge for packing. Please send a stamped addressed envelope for the latest list, or if resident abroad, an international reply coupon or UK postage stamps.

I also provide an approval service of black and white plain backed postcards of trams, as well as commercials, and hold a stock of over 25,000. Prices of most of the plain backed ones vary between 50p & £2, and my only requirements are that customers pay my outward postage and return unwanted cards within a reasonable time (otherwise I don't know if they have got lost in the post!).

Bus tickets are also sent out on approval, and I have large quantities priced from 5p to £1. Some tram tickets are also available but at higher prices.

---

# ADAM GORDON PUBLICATIONS

### Kintradwell Farmhouse, Brora, Sutherland KW9 6LU
### Tel: 01408 622660
### Email: adam@adamgordon.freewire.co.uk